CHOCTAILS
AND DREAMS

THE JOURNEY OF THE COCKTAIL OBSESSED CHOCOLATIER

How I took my food business from kitchen table to national retailer.

To Simon.

My best friend, my drinking buddy, my rock. Without you none of this would exist.

CONTENTS

PREFACE

In May 2012 I decided to turn my occasional chocolate-making hobby into a full-time career. Six years later I found myself checking my emails on an hourly basis, waiting for a purchase order from John Lewis to arrive in my inbox. This felt like the big one. The one thing we'd been working towards for the previous six years. We were about to hit the big time.

This book is the story of how we got to that point, and why we decided never to do it again.

When I say we, I'm talking about my husband Simon and I. Although I've been responsible for the day-to-day running of the business, and all the chocolate production, it's always been 'our' business. The cocktail-flavoured-chocolate concept was Simon's idea, and a lot of the key decisions we've made along the way have been down to him. He's certainly given me a sense of perspective and kept my feet firmly on the ground throughout.

I've written the book in the style of a memoir, because that's essentially what it is. However, it includes a lot of the key hints and tips, and a number of pitfalls to look out for along the way, for any of you thinking about setting up your own food-based business from home. If you're only interested in the business advice and not the back story, skip straight to Chapter Eight.

Each chapter is interspersed with a cocktail recipe, as chocolates based entirely on cocktails and drinks is our unique selling point (USP). I've only included recipes corresponding to the chocolates in our collections.

CHAPTER ONE

Chocolate and Childhood

My mum craved Mars Bars when she was pregnant with me. She also craved Piccalilli. Was it coincidence that my palate has always been for sweet or sour flavours? There was the day I requested vinegar sandwiches for tea. Lamb was my favourite roast because I could have a large dollop of mint sauce on the side. Fish and chips were always better in a tray than on a paper because I could get more vinegar on them that way. And then there was chocolate. The rich, sweet, delicious flavour. I would eat chocolate in the same way that Charlie Bucket did in Charlie and the Chocolate Factory – one tiny piece at a time, letting it slowly melt on my tongue with my eyes closed in reverence.

All children love chocolate. That's a given. Tests have proved that 15-16 weeks after conception a foetus will swallow more amniotic fluid when it's sweet and less when it's bitter, so my love of chocolate may be innate, as opposed to a correlation with mum's craving. However, I couldn't be fobbed off with any old chocolate. I didn't like Wagon Wheels because the chocolate didn't "feel" right in my mouth. Those pretty-looking chocolate drops with the hundreds and thousands sprinkled on the top always looked inviting, but the flavour always disappointed. Asking to lick the bowl of melted Scotbloc baking chocolate once mum was finished was a promise that never quite delivered.

One of my favourite childhood Christmas presents was a tiny vending machine which dispensed Cadbury's chocolate squares for a penny, but with only a limited supply of chocolate squares, I had to discipline myself to no more than one a day. When I was given a box of Roses as well I was delighted, as I could pick the Cadbury squares out and refill my machine. The joy of putting the penny in and having a chocolate delivered to me was almost as sweet as eating the chocolate itself.

Much as I loved chocolate, it was never an everyday thing. I would often make my stash of Christmas chocolates last until Easter. My weekend pocket money wasn't an immediate licence to buy chocolate as I might be saving up for something special instead. However, on a reasonably regular basis I remember my brother Christopher taking me to the local sweet shop (The Chocolate Box) on a Saturday afternoon where I would pick a treat. A quarter of Pineapple Chunks was a regular purchase, but I vividly remember the Bournville Sandwich; a small bar of about 8 squares with a layer of dark chocolate sandwiched between two layers of milk chocolate. We'd then head back home and enjoy our sweets in front of Saturday afternoon TV – Big Daddy versus Giant Haystacks being one of our highlights.

And then Easter would roll around and suddenly Cream Eggs would be in the shops. My brother was a "two bites, two sucks, and shove the rest in" kind of consumer. I was much more reverential, partly because I was too small to get the entire thing in my mouth in one go, but I wanted to make the experience last as long as possible, so I would nibble and lick my way through until I had that one last piece of delicious Cadbury's chocolate left to melt slowly on my tongue.

There was always a big tin of Quality Street at Christmas for the family to share. We never knew when the tape would be peeled off and we would be allowed to dive in, but we sat in anticipation, planning which flavour we were going to have first. As Christmas wore on it became more difficult to find your favourite flavour, desperately shaking the tin to see if something acceptable would pop up.

One occasion sits vividly in my memory. Dad was home from his pharmacy, exhausted after a day of dealing with winter coughs and colds. As usual he'd swapped his shoes for slippers and his jacket for a cardigan but still wore his shirt and tie, collar buttoned tight. We'd dined at six, as we always did, and were relaxing in front of the television. I opened the Quality Street tin to discover nothing but coconut ones left. No Toffee Pennies, no Green Triangles, no Orange Creams. Even a Coffee Cream would have been better than the strange tasting coconut sweet with the weird texture. I put the lid back on with a sigh. The resulting explosion that hit me made me jump with fright

11

— that stomach-dropping, flesh-tingling, heart-pounding adrenaline sensation — and I knew I was in some serious trouble. I had been rewarded with the sharp end of Dad's wrath for only wanting to eat the nice flavours. Food wasn't a commodity that we threw away, ever. I was sent to bed immediately. I couldn't quite fathom why I was in so much trouble, but once I'd got over the shock of the whole incident I cried myself to sleep.

I woke the following morning to discover my stuffed toys sitting in a circle on my bedroom floor, each with an empty coconut sweet wrapper in front of them. Dad was never big on face-to-face apologies (at least, I think it was an apology, as opposed to "See, *they've* eaten them you faddy child!").

Mum had her annual birthday box of Thornton's Continentals and they were *her* chocolates. They always looked so beautiful, luxurious, and grown up. We felt incredibly privileged and extremely grateful if Mum decided to share them around. I remember on one occasion feeling a rising panic that I might not get my favourite Vanilla Truffle as my sister Philippa deliberated over the box.

Dad, being a local business man (he owned and ran the village pharmacy) was given regular 'thank you' gifts from customers and suppliers. That was my first experience of liqueur chocolates. I never really enjoyed anything other than the Bailey's chocolate, but that never stopped me giving them a try! The sugar crunch was always welcome after the burn of rum or brandy – a spoonful of sugar helps the medicine go down, after all.

As I grew older my tastes changed and became more sophisticated. In my early twenties, I found high cocoa content dark chocolate (70% cocoa and above) far too bitter for my palate, but by the time I reached my thirties I found the taste much more appealing. Cadbury's was always my go-to chocolate but I've loved Lindor truffles since their launch in the mid-1980s, and Lindt bars were my indulgent treat throughout the 1990s. I began to enjoy darker chocolate more and with the bean-to-bar trend, which began in the late 1990s, I began to realise that chocolate from different countries had different flavour profiles. Ecuador was an immediate favourite of mine with its fruity notes.

Whilst my chocolate business was still in its infancy, I came across a 100% Ecuadorian chocolate, which was, and still is, one of the most extraordinarily divine chocolate experiences I've had. I was astounded when a few months later I tried a 100% Madagascan chocolate and discovered a completely different flavour experience. That led me down a dark chocolate path that I'm going to be following for many years to come.

The last time I had Cadbury's chocolate was about twelve months after Kraft took over the business and changed the Cream Egg recipe. At first I thought my palate had grown so used to "good" and "expensive" brands that it had affected the taste, but further investigation showed me that the base recipe had changed. No longer creamy and dreamy, the chocolate was powdery and had a taste of butyric acid – the chemical found in rancid butter, parmesan cheese, and the same chemical that gives vomit its very distinctive smell and acrid taste. It was the same type of chocolate that I'd experienced when in America and not the luxurious Dairy Milk I was used to. That was the moment when I realised I was in real danger of becoming a chocolate snob!

There was no doubt that I was always fascinated by chocolate and always treated it with reverence. Well, almost always. I have to admit to once swallowing an entire tube of Smarties in one go, and a packet of Munchies will hardly touch the sides, but the discovery of a new type of chocolate bar is a beautiful and exciting thing.

I can plot my life through chocolate bars from the Curly Wurly, through the Blue Riband, the United Bar with its candy crisp layer, Mars and Milky Way, the Secret, the Wispa, the Spira, the Galaxy Flake, the Boost Bar. When it comes to biscuits the Milk Chocolate Digestive gets my vote every time.

Mention the Freddo bar, the Caramac or the Pink Panther bar and I'm immediately back at a certain stage of my childhood. Walnut Whips, Turkish Delight and Double Deckers always remind me of mum and I enjoying a treat whilst waiting in the car for one of my siblings to finish an after-school club (I never understood why mum liked Turkish Delight or Fry's Chocolate Cream so much, or why dad thought that Easter egg chocolate was the best chocolate of all). Mars Bars were my favourite throughout high school (along with salt and vinegar crisps). Wispa bars remind me of university days. Twix, Secret, Boost and Toffee Poppets remind me of different work places. Barry Callebaut or Cacao Barry reminds me I have work to do….

Bucks Fizz

The drink is named after London's Buck's Club, where it was invented as an excuse to begin drinking early; it was first served in 1921 by a barman named Malachy McGarry. Traditionally, it is made by mixing two parts champagne and one part orange juice. Some older recipes list grenadine as an additional ingredient but the International Bartenders Association recipe does not include it. The original Buck's Club recipe is said to contain ingredients known only to the club's bartenders.

Ingredients	○ 5 cl (1 part) orange juice ○ 10 cl (2 parts) Champagne
Preparation	Pour the orange juice into a Champagne flute and top up with Champagne. Stir gently, garnish and serve.

CHAPTER TWO

Choosing a Career Path

I don't think Chocolatier ever figured in my list of things I wanted to be when I grew up, even though Charlie and the Chocolate Factory was one of my favourite books. I don't remember having any burning ambitions, come to think of it. I remember laying on the floor under my tiny chair during grands prix Sundays, aged about six or seven, and pretending to be a mechanic, "tinkering" under the seat. Astronaut struck a chord for a while, until in 1986 I realised just how dangerous that could be. Fashion Designer dropped in for a while in my early teens when I found I enjoyed needlework and knitting, before dropping out again when I realised I wasn't particularly gifted. I did my post O-Level work experience in a junior school and although I enjoyed my time there very much, I wasn't sure I wanted to do that for my entire working life. Two weeks had shown me just how unpredictable and exhausting little people can be.

The school careers chat was possibly one of the most depressing meetings of my life. A middle-aged spinster with large glasses, grey cardigan and sensible shoes asked me what I wanted to do. At the time I had no idea. I didn't even have anything far-fetched in my mind – the kind of career a teenager is too scared to voice in case they get laughed at. When I couldn't answer that question she asked what my parents did for a living (Dad was a Self-Employed Pharmacist and Mum had been a Music Teacher) and suggest I follow one of those paths. Admittedly that was probably borne out of me not having a clue what I wanted to be, but there was no productive discussion around what I thought might suit me.

At school I was one of the average kids. I didn't really shine at anything, but I was okay at most subjects. I enjoyed all the creative subjects – art, music, needlework – and I loved science. I was quite adept at making up excuses to get me out of games lessons, but I didn't think that was going to lead to a career of any prosperity.

When it came to choosing O-Level options, I had a huge dilemma. We were given a limited number of option streams (from memory I think it was nine). By this time I loved all three sciences and had a leaning (or at least a nudging) towards going into pharmacy to follow in my father's footsteps. I also loved art, but the only way I could take art O-Level was to drop at least one of the sciences. After several lengthy chats with various people, I went for the three sciences option. It was the 'sensible' choice if I was serious about Pharmacy (I wasn't sure that I was, but I had nothing else). Besides, "you won't ever find a career that combines art and science".

Still not knowing what I wanted to do once I'd completed my O-Levels, I studied Chemistry, Physics and Maths at A-Level (by this time I'd fallen out of love with Biology, and my "enthusiasm" for pharmacy had waned), and eventually settled on studying Chemistry at University because it was my favourite subject. Three years later I left the University of East Anglia with a 3rd Class Batchelor of Science in Chemistry, a thorough knowledge of all the 365 Norwich pubs which existed at the time, and still absolutely no idea what I wanted to do. I'd had it drilled into me from an early age that if I had a degree I could do anything I wanted. People would fall over themselves to offer me a job because I now had a "trained brain", so all I had to do was work out what I wanted to do.

I looked at working in the chemical industry, in FMCG, and in retail, thinking I could fall into one of the graduate training programmes, but I lacked the work experience they were looking for ("but my dad said all I needed was a degree…."). It turns out that being a Saturday girl from age fourteen in your father's pharmacy doesn't really cut it in the work experience stakes. I looked at becoming a medical rep and got pipped at the post on the two occasions I made it through to the final selection.

With no one bending over backwards to offer me a job, I took a temporary Christmas post with our local Boots the Chemist store. My section was the chocolate aisle. I had to make sure that the shelves were kept stocked throughout the day, making myself and my chocolate chariot as unobtrusive as possible to the shoppers. I thoroughly enjoyed those few weeks. I was constantly busy and I loved the camaraderie amongst the staff. Plus, I was working with chocolate. I was stunned at just how much chocolate we sold over those few weeks. In the last few days before the Christmas break I was constantly replenishing the shelves. By the time I'd got to the end of the section I needed to go back to the beginning and start all over again. Christmas it seems, is a key chocolate occasion.

I stayed within retail for the next few years (mostly selling wines and spirits), until I decided I needed a new challenge and moved into direct sales, then account management, and from there into recruitment, where I eventually ended up placing myself into a marketing support role in a recruitment agency, which sounded fascinating from the moment I saw the job spec. Marketing had often interested me but whilst the majority of my roles had included a marketing element, I lacked any direct strategic experience to apply for a pure marketing role. When the job spec landed on my desk I knew I would be perfect for the role. It was a step away from the front line into something more creative, and with first-hand knowledge of what a Recruitment Consultant needs and wants, it wasn't difficult to sell myself into the role.

As an aside, at this time I was living in Birmingham and my train commute took me past the back of the Cadbury's factory in Bournville. Although I couldn't ask the train to slow down, I was just like Charlie Bucket in that I would hold my nose high in the air and take long deep sniffs of the gorgeous chocolatey smell as we went past. I systematically took friends and family to the factory for a day out to experience the tour, the free samples and the outlet store. The section which fascinated me the most was the handmade chocolates, watching people tempering on a huge marble slab, and others hand-dipping and decorating the confectionery.

Marketing continued to be my main career focus for several years. Having been made redundant from the recruitment support role, I decided to leave Birmingham in early 2003 and take up a similar role with a small recruitment agency in Mayfair. I'd met Simon by this time and thought there might be some longevity in our relationship. Even though we were both getting back on our feet after going through divorces and he had two young children to consider, there was a spark between us we didn't want to ignore. We connected on so many levels. Simon was (and still is) an IT Consultant in London, so I decided to see if the streets really were paved in gold and headed for the capital myself. I was the one without any ties, so it was up to me to make the move.

May 2003 was a major turning point in my life. I was right about the longevity, and moved in with Simon on May 4th. I also took a job as a Marketing Executive with PriceWaterhouseCoopers in London later that same month. It was a varied role, providing internal and external marketing support to my team, until the CRM training aspect became my entire focus. I'd been tasked with helping people to navigate around the new Client Relationship Management database as part of my role from day one. Gradually I was spending more and more time helping people update their contacts on the database, running lunch and learn sessions and full-day training programmes until I became the dedicated CRM Trainer for the Audit team. I particularly enjoyed the creativity of developing training materials. I also loved the autonomy the role afforded me and I thoroughly enjoyed being an expert in my field.

Cosmopolitan

The International Bartenders Association recipe is based on vodka citron. The cosmopolitan is a relative of cranberry coolers and bears a likeness in composition to the kamikaze cocktail.

The origin of the Cosmopolitan cocktail is disputed. While the cocktail is widely perceived to be a modern creation, there is a strikingly similar recipe which appears in Pioneers of Mixing at Elite Bars 1903-1933, published in 1934.

Ingredients	o 4cl Vodka Citron o 1.5cl Cointreau o 1.5cl Fresh Lime Juice o 3cl Cranberry Juice
Preparation	Shake all ingredients in a cocktail shaker filled with ice. Strain into a large cocktail glass. Garnish with a lime slice.

CHAPTER THREE

How It All Began

Chocolate-making started as a hobby for me in the early 1990s. It was just a whim I had one day. I liked being creative in the kitchen. Cakes have never been wholly successful for me, plus I'm not a big cake eater, so they would often go stale before we could finish them. I enjoyed making biscuits and desserts, but for some reason I decided I'd make some truffles. I found a recipe in my Good Housekeeping cookbook for rich chocolate rum truffles:

- 225g plain chocolate
- 2 egg yolks
- 25g butter
- 10ml rum
- 15ml single cream
- Drinking chocolate powder

At the time I thought the amount of rum was on the stingy side, but I followed the recipe to the letter and produced some reasonably pleasant chocolate truffles. They didn't taste of rum, but they were certainly rich and chocolatey and very simple to make, melting the chocolate and cream together and then blending everything to a smooth emulsion before rolling them into balls and dusting them in cocoa powder.

Having made rum truffles I tried brandy and also whisky and failed to tell the difference between the different flavours. At this point, I adapted the original recipe. I left out the egg yolks as I was now overrun with egg whites and there's only so much meringue a person can consume. The omission of the eggs didn't seem to have any detrimental effect on the final product.

I added a bit more alcohol. In fact I added quite a lot more alcohol and eventually worked out the optimum ratio to give the truffles a nice soft texture but not too much that they became over-sticky and lost their shape. It was considerably more than 5ml per 100g of chocolate. I kept the cream in for a while but eventually omitted that as well. Yes, it gave a slightly creamier texture to the finished product, but by leaving out the fresh cream I got a longer shelf life. It's only now, when I look back to these annual sessions, that I realise I was already tinkering with product development.

My chocolate truffles became an essential part of Christmas celebrations for the next few years. I would generally stick to six flavours – rum, brandy, whisky, Baileys, Tia Maria and vanilla. I tried dipping the truffles (covering them in a layer of chocolate) with varying degrees of success, sometimes having to cover up what I now know are spots of sugar bloom or fat bloom. Rolling the truffles in cocoa powder, sugar, or chocolate shavings gave them a much more consistent appearance, although I longed to get that professional look. However, family and friends enjoyed them to the point that their eyes would light up when they saw them again.

I tried to make moulded truffles using an ice cube tray but most of the chocolates stuck to the tray and wouldn't set in the fridge, or even freezer. I had no idea why and I now had a gooey mess that became dessert for the next few evenings. I abandoned the moulded truffle idea and continued with rolled truffles.

I'd not made any truffles for a few years, when in 2009 a PwC away-day took us on a chocolate-themed tour of London, followed by an afternoon of chocolate making. As I've got a peanut intolerance I was given my own set of ingredients and equipment, and placed at the end of the table near the organisers, well away from the peanut brittle. That was my first serious chocolate conversation. I wanted to know what caused the strange spots on chocolate, why it didn't always set, and a plethora of other questions.

I learned about tempering chocolate, and had the process explained to me. It was a little more involved than just melting chocolate over a bowl of hot water as I had been doing. The afternoon reawakened my enjoyment of chocolate-making, and I resolved to make some truffles again before too long.

Three chocolate gifts were now standing in the way of me taking up the hobby regularly again.

The first gift was from my brother-in-law and his girlfriend at the time, who gave me a Hotel Chocolat bar selection, 50% of which were nut-based (did I mention my peanut intolerance and general dislike of any nutty flavours at any point in our years of knowing each other?) I couldn't really blame my brother-in-law for the oversight. His girlfriend had taken control of present purchasing and was one of those people who talked more than she listened.

The second gift was a small box of chocolates from one of the school mums, who couldn't make it to one of our parties. She dropped a box of chocolates round with an apology that they'd had a last-minute change of plan. It was a beautiful, artisan box of handmade chocolates. The box was as pretty as the chocolates inside. Again, around 50% were nut-based, so I picked out the ones I liked and handed the rest around. I couldn't help thinking it was such a shame that I could never finish a box of chocolates I'd been given.

The third gift was a Charbonnel & Walker heart-shaped box I bought for Simon and I to share on Valentine's Day 2010. I'd walked past the shop on Liverpool Street Station on many occasions. I loved the luxurious packaging and salivated over the beautifully displayed chocolate. I spent £15 on the pre-selected box, and of the nine chocolates inside …. four were nut-based. Simon always teases me about the fact that he's made to eat the nut chocolates when he really wanted the salted caramels, the whisky truffles, the orange creams. I no longer had enough stuffed toys to step in and eat them for me. I felt guilty, disappointed and ripped off. It wasn't the romantic sit-down-and-share-a-box-of-chocolates-on-the-sofa end to the day that I'd hoped.

There was nothing for it. I was going to have to make chocolates again. Just for us.

Harvey Wallbanger

The Harvey Wallbanger appears in literature as early as 1971. The cocktail is reputed to have been invented in 1952 by three-time world champion mixologist Donato "Duke" Antone and named after a surfer frequenting Antone's bar. However, recent research casts doubt on this theory.

Other historians emphasise the role of the McKesson Imports Company and its marketing team for developing the drink. It is known that McKesson executive George Bednar was instrumental in promoting the drink as a means of selling its component Galliano liqueur.

Ingredients	o 4.5cl Vodka o 1.5cl Galliano o 9cl Fresh Orange Juice
Preparation	Stir the vodka and orange juice with ice in a highball glass then float the Galliano on top. Garnish and serve.

CHAPTER FOUR

The Chocolate Hobbyist

My Saturday afternoons were now turned over to chocolate making, and I would spend an hour or so in the kitchen before dinner preparations began. My weekly shop always included a quantity of 200g bars of own-brand chocolate. I started with the original six flavours I'd made all those years ago, and also added Chambord and Cointreau to my repertoire. The truffle mix was rolled into balls, dipped in melted chocolate and then rolled in cocoa powder, chocolate flakes and other decorations. They had a rustic hand-made appearance, but they were just for us and tasted fine, so I didn't get too preoccupied with the overall look of them.

I then decided to have a go at a Strawberry and Champagne truffle. I made this using white chocolate in the same ratio as I'd done with the dark chocolate, and initially I couldn't understand why the truffle mix wouldn't set. It was the first time I'd tried making a truffle in white chocolate; everything else had been in dark chocolate. After a few failed attempts, I decided that the only way forward was to try moulded chocolates. This is where you create a chocolate shell in a mould, pipe in the filling and then cap off with another layer of chocolate. I purchased a set of silicone moulds from Amazon and the result was passable. They were individual moulds as opposed to a tray, so I could make a small quantity at a time instead of fifteen to twenty in one go.

The Strawberry and Champagne truffle still exists in Choctails standard range. We called it 'Mixed Doubles' as a nod to the tennis season. The ingredients are a little more sophisticated than the original blend I put together, but it's essentially the same recipe.

The introduction of the silicone moulds meant the fillings could be a little 'wetter' than I needed them to be for rolled truffles, which also meant I could add more alcohol to the dark chocolate blends, hence why our Whisky and Rum truffles in particular pack such a punch.

It was at this point that Simon asked "could you put a cocktail flavour into chocolate?" The idea intrigued me as it was something I'd not come across before. I spent a few days researching recipes from our cocktail book selection and decided it was worth a try. That casual question, which turned out to be an excuse to spend an afternoon drinking cocktails, was the inception of our chocolate business.

And so began a blissful Saturday afternoon of drinking cocktails and eating chocolate. We'd even planned ahead with dinner bubbling away in the slow cooker. By the end of the session I thought we might be on to something. Unfortunately we'd failed to write a single thing down, so we had to do it all over again. Life can be tough sometimes.

Over time we worked our way through our favourite cocktails. Some worked as a chocolate, some didn't. The Long Island Iced Tea went through many iterations over several years before it was allowed into the final selection, and didn't make it in until we rebranded some years later. I would regularly revisit the idea only to find it never quite tasted right. I do remember the Cosmopolitan was one of our initial successes. Although I didn't realise it at the time, I was already going through a thorough R&D process whenever we decided to try to make a new cocktail-flavoured chocolate. There was a small seed being incubated that eventually, inevitably, became a bone fide business concept.

My aim, from day one, was to make a chocolate that tasted as close as possible to the original cocktail, and not just to make a ganache by blending chocolate with a ready-mixed cocktail.

The first thing we needed to do was mix the cocktail. That in itself can be a challenge as there can often be many different versions circulating in various cocktail books and on various online platforms. The three cocktail books I owned at the time gave me three different Woo Woo recipes, for example. We stick to Difford's Guide or the International Bartender's Guide now.

Now we have to taste the cocktail. And I mean really taste. It's a lot like wine tasting, identifying all the flavour profiles in the drink. I take a lot of notes whilst I'm doing this.

Next we introduce the chocolate element. Does the flavour work best with white, milk or dark chocolate? As a rule of thumb I only use white or dark for the centre of the chocolate. I rarely use milk chocolate in my truffle blend, although there are some exceptions. That decided, we blend the cocktail as it is in the glass with the chosen chocolate to make a ganache.

Now we taste again. What has the chocolate done to the flavour of the cocktail? Can we still taste all the elements of the drink? Are any of the flavours enhanced? Are any of the flavours masked? This is where I get to be a Chemist again, trying different flavour blends and ingredients to try and mimic the original cocktail. It all needs to be done systematically and everything needs to be written down because the one time you forget to make notes is the day you get everything just right first time.

Looking back, I never once thought this was an awful lot of work just to make chocolates for home consumption. I was loving spending a few hours every week experimenting, tinkering, creating. It's so true that great accomplishments depend not so much on ingenuity as on hard work.

Once we were happy with the ganache filling, I could start to make some test batches. In some cases we already knew what the chocolate shell was going to be. The Pina Colada, for example, is a cream-based cocktail, so we use white chocolate to mimic the cream element. Whilst the truffle might taste very nice in a dark chocolate shell, there's no way it's going to taste like a Pina Colada.

A lot of the time we had no idea which chocolate was going to make the best shell, so we would end up making three different batches (with the recent development of the Ruby Chocolate grade, there's now potential for a fourth batch), and seeing which one gave the best flavour profile.

There are occasions when we really can't decide the best combination. The Singapore Sling worked equally well as a dark chocolate centre in a white chocolate shell as it did with the white chocolate centre in the dark chocolate shell. We put it to a public vote and it came out as 52% in favour of the dark shell.

The next step is testing. Yes, I do mean testing it on the public and yes, we get a lot of people offering to help out with this part of the process. Monday morning meetings at PwC were much brighter when I'd been experimenting. Feedback isn't always what you hope for though. "These are lovely" is great to hear, but the person who shrieks "oh my god, this tastes just like a Woo Woo!" is much more helpful. Even more helpful are the comments like "I don't taste the Martini Rosso in the Manhattan" or "It's nice but I can't tell what cocktail it's supposed to be". That's honest feedback and not just someone who's excited about free chocolate.

Now that I was giving chocolate to people other than us, I needed to get a proper grip on why the chocolate didn't always look great and went back to the conversation I'd had on the away day about tempering chocolate. I'd been following the process but I'd forgotten the temperatures I needed to achieve at each stage. As with everything these days, the Internet is a mine of information but can also be a minefield. I found a step-by-step guide on how to temper chocolate and followed the process. It was only when everything went horribly wrong that I realised I was on an American site and the temperatures were in Fahrenheit and not Centigrade. The thick, muddy and lumpy mess couldn't be salvaged and ended up in the food-recycling caddy.

Tempering chocolate is done to pre-crystallise the cocoa butter in it and ensures the cocoa butter takes on a stable crystalline form. It's an essential step for making smooth, glossy, evenly-coloured chocolate, and prevents the dull grey colour and waxy texture that happens when the cocoa fat separates out (fat bloom). Tempered chocolate has a crisp, satisfying snap.

Tempering also takes a lot of practice. I tried the microwave method for smaller quantities, and that worked reasonably well, but it was all too easy to burn the chocolate by overheating it. The process involves heating the chocolate buttons or pieces in short bursts (20 to 30 seconds) and then agitating the chocolate until the point where it's almost melted, but still with some solid pieces in the bowl, then stirring vigorously to allow the residual heat to melt the final chocolate pieces. It's a process that takes time and can create hot spots in the chocolate, which will burn. Now you're left with a smoky microwave, a ruined batch of chocolate at best, a burned plastic bowl at worst, and have to start again.

I hankered after a marble slab, but as I didn't have one, I discovered the seed method was the one that suited me best, adding solid chocolate pieces to a bowl of melted chocolate to bring the temperature down and stirring to ensure the crystals form in the right way, before bringing the temperature back up to the optimum working temperature. I was glad of my scientific training to help me understand the theory – after 25 years I was finally using my Chemistry degree!

It took a while to master the process, and there were still many disastrous results ahead, but my chocolates began to look a little more professional and a little less 'home made'.

Manhattan

Popular history suggests that the drink originated at the Manhattan Club in New York City in the early 1870s, where it was invented by Dr. Iain Marshall for a banquet. The success of the banquet made the drink fashionable, prompting several people to request the drink by referring to the name of the club where it originated. However, there are prior references to various similar cocktail recipes called "Manhattan" and served in the Manhattan area. The original "Manhattan cocktail" was a mix of "American Whiskey, Italian Vermouth and Angostura bitters". During Prohibition Canadian whisky was primarily used because it was available.

Ingredients	○ 5cl Rye Whiskey ○ 2cl Sweet Red Vermouth ○ Dash Angostura Bitters
Preparation	Stir over ice and strain into a cocktail glass.

CHAPTER FIVE

Getting More Serious

Over the weeks, I introduced more and more flavours to our range. The Kir Royale took a while to perfect, as it initially tasted more like Ribena than a sophisticated cocktail. The Tequila and Lime, which eventually became the Margarita, worked beautifully first time.

Whenever we went out I would pore over the cocktail menu for inspiration. I couldn't pass by an off-licence without popping in to peruse the spirits and liqueurs range, searching for unusual ingredients and new ideas. My weekly shop clanked a lot more and the glass recycling box was almost always full.

In February 2011 my stepson Charlie did two weeks work experience at a local dental laboratory. It wasn't his first choice for work experience, but it was only a five minute bike ride away, meaning he got a longer lie-in than his classmates. He enjoyed the camaraderie, and the fact that they had the radio on all day meant the atmosphere was more relaxed than he'd originally envisaged.

During his second week, Charlie asked if he could take some of my chocolates in to work with him. Other members of staff had brought occasional treats in, so he wanted to follow suit. I packed a few chocolates into a Tupperware box and thought, at best, people would think they were charming.

That evening I returned from my daily London commute to a breathless and very excited boy whose words cascaded out of his mouth so fast that I had to ask him to repeat the entire story.

The son of one of the management team had popped into the lab and tried some of my chocolate. He just happened to work at our prestigious local department store and his feedback was that my chocolates were good enough for them to stock in the store.

Sorry, what?

I currently make about twenty to fifty chocolates over a weekend for personal consumption and you're saying I could retail them?

After I'd finished hyperventilating I began to think logically. We're not currently in a position to do this, but we could be.

Looking back, Charlie was the catalyst that turned me from chocolate hobbyist to potential business owner. I was also extremely flattered and humbled when he used me as a case study in an A-Level Economics project a couple of years later.

We'd already got the name. "Choctails" had popped into my head one afternoon as a brand name. It summed us up perfectly – a combination of chocolate and cocktails (someone subsequently pointed out that "Cocklets" wouldn't have had the same appeal….), but we had no brand identity. Everything up until now had been pie-in-the-sky "Could you imagine if we turned this into a business …?" and not "Can you imagine when…". I'd been in marketing for the last few years, and I'd recently

47

completed a marketing degree through work, so I had some basic brand training. How difficult could it be to develop a Choctails brand? I opted for a simple design – too simple, although I didn't know it at the time. I decided on a burgundy and white colour scheme with the word 'Choctails' in Algerian font.

I made my first serious equipment purchase and bought a table-top tempering machine. It could only temper small quantities of chocolate, but it was big enough for my current requirements. The automatic tempering machine goes through the same process as I was already doing by hand, but the only input I have is when it beeps and I need to move it to the next stage. I was using a machine which could prepare just under a kilo of chocolate. The chocolate goes into a dry-heated bowl and once it's all been melted, the machine beeps for me to add some fresh chocolate buttons, just as I would when I'm seeding the chocolate. None of that tedious melting and stirring.

I then began to play around with different flavour ideas and techniques – Chilli Chocolate, a Balsamic Truffle (a definite throwback to my love of acidic flavours), Turkish Delight, Caramels.

We began to hatch a plan to start selling our chocolates to the public. Simon is a Software Developer and was confident he could pull together a simple website using PayPal to take payments. Choctails.co.uk was already registered to someone in the Netherlands, but was due for renewal in October. Choctails.com was owned by an American company selling cupcakes. Choctails.org.uk was available, however, so we registered that, figuring it was better to have something than nothing at all.

We narrowly missed out on .co.uk on that occasion. Having made a mental note to check back on October 24 we got side-tracked and didn't check until a few days later, to discover someone in Doncaster had purchased the licence for two years. That was a bit of a blow at the time.

By Christmas I had a reasonable range of flavours, and of course the family were given Choctails as part of their presents.

Simon then suggested to me that he send me on a chocolate course for my birthday present, so in February 2012 I headed off to Banbury to the Callebaut Chocolate Academy for a two-day Introduction to Chocolate Making course.

The Chocolate Academy have a plethora of courses available, covering various chocolate and patisserie techniques, and in recent years have also introduced a course aimed specifically at people who want to set up their own chocolate business. Unfortunately that was long after I'd set up in business myself, so I wasn't able to take advantage of that particular course.

The UK Chocolate Academy centre is a state of the art, purpose-built training environment, adjacent to the Barry Callebaut factory. I was staying at the nearby Holiday Inn, so walked the short distance to the factory. As I arrived at the gates, feeling a little nervous, the familiar smell of melted chocolate hit me, and my anxiety immediately melted away.

We were shown into a classroom where we were all introduced to the teaching staff, each other, and the head of Callebaut UK. In the most part, our course was made up of serious hobbyists, with a small group, such as myself, thinking about possibly, potentially, maybe, one day, setting up a chocolate business.

After an introductory film delving into how chocolate is made, we donned our chef's whites and hair nets and were shown into the gleaming training room, where it was time to get our hands dirty.

I was taken right back to basics. Much as I'd taught myself how to temper chocolate through books, online videos and troubleshooting sites, I still hadn't been able to get great results every time. We watched as chocolate was tempered on a marble slab, and then were each assigned a work station with a large chocolate holding tank. We first learned how to temper using the seed method. Initially we were given a thermometer to help us, but Beverley, our tutor, announced she would be taking the thermometers away.

Okay, how am I supposed to do this without a thermometer?

It turns out that thermometers can give you a false sense of security, as other factors, such as humidity, can come into play. It's more about how the chocolate looks and feels, and understanding the consistency at each stage of the process. I suddenly began to feel like a serious chocolatier.

The key things I learned over the two days were:

1. Pouring chocolate into cold moulds doesn't help the chocolate set quicker, as I'd previously thought; it shocks the chocolate and doesn't give it the proper retraction allowing it to un-mould easily ("ahhhhh," I said, enlightened).

2. Pre-brushing the mould helps get the chocolate into the nooks and crannies which means less chance of air bubbles and a more attractive finished product (Note to self: buy some new paint brushes when I get home).

3. When mixed with cream, or any other liquid, the cocoa solids in melted chocolate help absorb the liquid creating a thick mixture that will firm up. Due to the absence of cocoa solids in white chocolate, less liquid is required for the ganache to set (which explained why the original strawberry and cream ganache was so runny and sent me down the moulded chocolate path).

4. Polycarbonate moulds give a better finish than silicone and are much more hard wearing (I was sensing a serious shopping spree coming on).

Over two intensive and thoroughly enjoyable days we made moulded chocolates, dipped pralines, hollow figures, and chocolate lollipops. My techniques improved dramatically. My biggest problem was transporting everything home on the train … Actually, that was my second biggest problem; my biggest problem was having to go back to my day job on Thursday when all I wanted to do was gaze into a tank of chocolate …

I felt unbelievably flat as I left the house on Thursday morning and headed to London. It was instantly made worse by the fact that a new directive had been brought in, which meant I could only work from home one day per week by prior agreement. Simon and I had planned to share childcare duties over half term with him working from home Monday and Tuesday, and me taking over for the remaining three days, but when I presented the idea to my line manager, I received short shrift. It was one day from home and take the remainder as holiday. No negotiation.

In a fit of pique I booked the entire week off, ordered a chocolate holding tank, and placed my first order for chocolate ingredients from Keylink – the chocolate supplier recommended by the UK Chocolate Academy, and one I still use to this day.

Over half term week I had a blast creating new flavour ideas. That was the week I developed the Pina Colada, the Harvey Wallbanger and the Hurricane. Having been introduced to Callebaut's coloured and flavoured chocolate range I also started developing the Tequila Sunrise, the Strawberry Daiquiri and the Whisky Sour.

Work was beginning to get in the way of my chocolate making. My line manager was also on a mission to make my life miserable – it wasn't due to anything I'd done specifically, it was just my turn to bear the brunt. Having watched everyone else in the team go through it, I'd known it was just a matter of time before it was my turn. I found solace in chocolate.

My redundancy, when it came, was one of the best things that ever happened to me. Our department was having a reshuffle and every team member was to have an individual meeting with their line manager to discuss their future role. At a department night out on 22 March I realised that everyone who'd had their meeting to date had been offered voluntary redundancy. My meeting was the following day. I left the party early and went home to talk through the inevitable with Simon. He was so wonderfully supportive. We could manage on just his salary. It would mean a few sacrifices, but why didn't I just set up my chocolate business full time and avoid all the corporate angst?

It was all I could do not to laugh as the redundancy package was laid out in front of me. I knew the drill. I'd been through it a couple of times before in previous employments. The meeting room is usually one that's tucked out of the way, and definitely not on a main thoroughfare. There are usually two other people in the room with you. This time it was my line manager and a suited forty-something HR representative called Matthew, who looked terribly serious but managed a hint of sympathy in his expression.

My line manager opened with "We've called you here on a serious matter". I relaxed back into my chair, which seemed to throw him off a little. Sweat began to bead on his forehead, and he was reading out the preordained spiel staccato-fashion. He delivered the speech one painful word at a time, glancing up at me (actually, defocussing just over my shoulder) in-between each word.

I had to bite my lip on several occasions to stop myself laughing out loud, and at one point I could feel my shoulders were visibly shaking. I'm sure the HR representative must have thought I was insane, or that I just hadn't grasped what was going on. Trust me, I knew exactly what was going on. The man who had been making my life a misery for the previous two months had just enabled me to set up my own business. Had this been the motivation behind his attitude? That he didn't want to go through this excruciating scenario, hoping I'd hand my notice in first?

Needless to say, I accepted the offer, handed back my laptop and pass, said a reluctant goodbye to my work family, and stepped out into a whole new world.

Tequila Sunrise

The original Tequila Sunrise contained tequila, creme de cassis, lime juice and soda water, and was served at the Arizona Biltmore Hotel, where it was created by Gene Sulit in the 1930s.

The more popular modern version of the cocktail contains tequila, orange juice, and grenadine and was created by Bobby Lozoff and Billy Rice in the early 1970s while working as young bartenders at the Trident in Sausalito, California.

Ingredients	o 4.5cl Tequila o 9cl Orange Juice o 1.5cl Grenadine Syrup
Preparation	Pour the tequila and orange juice into a tall glass over ice. Add the grenadine, which will sink to the bottom. Stir gently to create the sunrise effect.

CHAPTER SIX

A Brief History of Chocolate

Before I continue my journey, I wanted to delve into the history of chocolate from its origins to the product it is today. When I first began working with chocolate, I was using supermarket own brand bars as they were affordable. Following my visit to the UK Chocolate Academy I discovered there were many different flavour profiles. I found out that the fluidity of the chocolate was a factor. I began working with larger volumes and buying specialist chocolate, which led me to look deeper into how chocolate was produced and what generated these differences.

Chocolate is made from the fruit of the cacao tree, native to Central and South America. It isn't clear when chocolate was first consumed, but ancient Olmec pots and vessels from around 1500 BC were discovered with traces of theobromine, which is a compound found in chocolate and tea.

It is believed the Olmecs used cacao to create a ceremonial drink, but it's unclear as to whether they used the bitter beans or the sweet pulp in their concoction.

The Olmecs undoubtedly passed their cacao knowledge on to the Mayans, who revered chocolate. The Mayan written history mentions chocolate drinks being used in celebrations and to finalise important transactions.

Chocolate was readily available to almost everyone in Mayan culture. In many households it was enjoyed with every meal. Mayan chocolate was thick and frothy and often combined with chilli pepper, honey or water, and similar to the modern Chilate drink native to Central America. Chilate is prepared from chilli pepper, roasted corn and cocoa with spices such as star anise, pepper, ginger and cinnamon.

The Aztecs believed cacao was given to them by their gods; that the seeds were the gift of Quetzalcoatl, the god of wisdom. The Aztecs were unable to grow cacao themselves, as their home in the Mexican highlands was unsuitable for it, so chocolate was a luxury imported into the empire. They enjoyed the spiced chocolate beverages in the same way the Mayans did, but they also used cacao beans as currency. Those who lived in areas ruled by the Aztecs were required to offer cacao seeds as a tax. The Aztecs used a currency system in which one turkey cost one hundred cacao beans and one fresh avocado was worth three beans. In Aztec culture cacao beans were considered more valuable than gold.

Aztec chocolate was mostly an upper-class extravagance with the lower classes enjoying it occasionally at weddings or other celebrations.

The Aztec ruler Montezuma II supposedly drank gallons of chocolate each day for energy and as an aphrodisiac. It's also said he reserved some of his cacao beans for his military.

At the Cadbury's factory tour there had been a section dedicated to the origins of chocolate and they had included a cold, bitter chocolate drink to sample, similar to the one the Aztecs would have consumed. At the time I had wondered just how something so bitter had given rise to something so sweet, delicious and indulgent.

There are conflicting reports about how chocolate arrived in Europe, although it is agreed that it first arrived in Spain at some point during the sixteenth century.

One story says Christopher Columbus discovered cacao beans after intercepting a trade ship on a journey to America and brought the beans back to Spain with him in 1502. A second states Spanish conquistador Hernan Cortes was introduced to chocolate by the Aztecs of Montezuma's court but kept his chocolate knowledge secret when he returned to Spain with his stash of beans. A third story suggests that friars who presented Guatemalan Mayans to Philip II of Spain in 1544 also brought cacao beans along as a gift.

After the Spanish conquest of the Aztecs, chocolate was introduced to court by the friars. Chocolate had made no impact in Europe until then. By the late 1500s chocolate was a much-loved indulgence by the Spanish court. It was still served as a beverage but the Spanish added sugar and honey to counteract the natural bitterness. As other European countries visited parts of Central America they also learned about cacao and brought chocolate back to their respective countries.

The Europeans sweetened the traditional bitter Aztec drink recipe and made their own varieties of hot chocolate with cane sugar, cinnamon and other common spices such as vanilla.

When chocolate first arrived in Europe it was a luxury only the rich could enjoy. Fashionable chocolate houses for the wealthy cropped up throughout London, Amsterdam and other European cities.

Chocolate-mania began to spread throughout Europe and with the high demand for chocolate came chocolate plantations, which were worked by thousands of slaves. Cacao plantations spread as the English, Dutch and French colonised and planted. With the depletion of Mesoamerican workers, largely to disease, cacao production was often the work of poor wage labourers and African slaves.

New processes that sped up the production of chocolate emerged early in the Industrial Revolution. In 1815, Dutch chemist Coenraad Johannes van Houten discovered a way to treat cacao beans with alkaline salts to make a powdered chocolate that was easier to mix with water and reduced its bitterness. The process became known as 'Dutch processing' and the chocolate produced was called cacao powder or 'Dutch cocoa'.

In 1828 Van Houten also invented the cocoa press to remove about half the natural fat (cocoa butter) from the chocolate liquor, which made chocolate both cheaper to produce and more consistent in quality.

Dutch processing and the chocolate press helped make chocolate affordable for everyone and opened the door for chocolate to be mass-produced, introducing the modern era of chocolate.

For most of the 19th century chocolate was enjoyed as a beverage mixed with milk or water until in 1847 British chocolatier JS Fry and Sons created the first chocolate bar moulded from a paste made of sugar, chocolate liquor and cocoa butter.

Swiss chocolatier Danier Peter is generally credited for adding dried milk powder to chocolate to create milk chocolate in 1876 but it wasn't until several years later that he worked with his friend Henri Nestlé, and as the Nestlé Company brought milk chocolate to the mass market.

These first chocolate bars were hard and difficult to chew. In 1879 another Swiss chocolatier Rudolph Lindt invented the conching machine which mixed and aerated chocolate giving it a smooth, melt-in-the-mouth consistency that blended well with other ingredients.

By the early 20th century, family chocolate companies such as Cadbury, Mars, Nestlé and Hershey were mass-producing a variety of chocolate confections to meet growing demand.

Shirley Temple

This non-alcoholic mixed drink was invented by a bartender at Chasen's restaurant in West Hollywood to serve to the then-child actress Shirley Temple.

Ingredients	o Splash of Grenadine Syrup o Glass of Ginger Ale
Preparation	Add a splash of grenadine to a glass of ginger ale and garnish with a maraschino cherry.

CHAPTER SEVEN

Modern Chocolate Production

Most modern chocolate is highly refined and mass-produced. Production costs can be, and are, decreased by reducing the amount of cocoa solids or by substituting cocoa butter with another fat such as palm oil. I've always refused to compromise on the quality of my chocolate, partly because it doesn't taste as good, but mainly because the cheaper products rely heavily on the addition of palm oil.

Modern-day chocolate production comes at a cost. Many cocoa farmers struggle to make ends meet and turn to low-wage or slave-labour (sometimes acquired by child trafficking) to stay competitive. This has prompted chocolate companies to reconsider how they get their cocoa supply. It has also resulted in appeals for more Fair Trade chocolate which is created in an ethical and sustainable way.

The production of cocoa begins in the tropical regions around the Equator where the hot and humid climate is well suited for growing cocoa trees. 70% of the world's cocoa beans now come from four West African countries – Ivory Coast, Ghana, Nigeria and Cameroon. The Ivory Coast and Ghana are the two largest producers, accounting for more than half of the world's cocoa. Cocoa is also grown in Indonesia, Brazil and Ecuador.

Worldwide, 90% of cocoa is grown on small family farms of two to five hectares with just 5% coming from large plantations of forty hectares or more. Cocoa production provides livelihoods for between forty and fifty million farmers, rural workers and their families in the Global South. In the Ivory Coast and Ghana up to 90% of the farmers rely on cocoa for their primary income.

Growing cocoa is hard manual work and very labour intensive, as caring for and harvesting the beans requires close and continuous attention.

The cocoa tree flowers and bears fruit throughout the year. It produces large cocoa pods which need to be cut from the trees by machetes or knocked off the tree with sticks. Each cocoa pod contains around twenty to thirty seeds sitting in a sweet white pulp. These seeds are the cocoa beans. It takes an entire year's crop from one tree to make half a kilo of cocoa.

As pods do not ripen at the same time the trees need to be monitored continuously. Cocoa is also a very delicate crop, easily affected by changes in weather and susceptible to diseases and pests. It is important to harvest the pods when they are fully ripe, because unripe beans will have a low cocoa butter content, or the sugars in the white pulp will be insufficient for fermentation, resulting in a weak flavour.

After the harvest the ripe pods need to be cut open with machetes, and the beans with their surrounding pulp are taken out. The cocoa beans then need to be fermented, dried and cleaned. The beans of the cacao tree have an intense bitter taste and must be fermented to develop the flavour.

The beans and pulp are placed in piles or bins, allowing them access to essential micro-organisms so that fermentation of the pectin-containing material can begin. Yeasts produce ethanol, lactic acid bacteria produce lactic acid, and acetic acid bacteria produce acetic acid. The fermentation process, which takes up to seven days, also produces several flavour precursors, eventually resulting in the familiar chocolate taste.

After fermentation the beans are dried quickly to prevent mould growth. Climate and weather permitting, this is done by spreading the beans out in the sun from five to seven days. The dried beans are transported to a chocolate-manufacturing facility. The beans are cleaned to remove twigs, stones and other debris. After cleaning, the beans are graded and packed. Once the beans are packed into cocoa sacks the farmers are ready to sell the product to intermediaries.

Since 2016 the producer price for a 64 kilogram bag of cocoa has been around £67. An organic and Fair Trade premium increases that price to £72.50. That equates to an annual salary for the average cocoa farmer of less than £2,000.

Intermediaries buy the sacks of unprocessed beans and sell them to exporters. When the beans reach the grinding companies in the Global North the cocoa then needs processing into chocolate.

The beans are roasted to develop their colour and flavour into what our modern palates expect from fine chocolate. The beans are crushed and the outer shell of the beans is removed. The inner cocoa bean meat is broken into small pieces called cocoa nibs. The cocoa nibs are then ground to cocoa mass. Cocoa Mass is unadulterated chocolate in its rough form. Once the cocoa mass is liquefied by heating it is called chocolate liquor. The resulting cocoa liquor is either used to manufacture chocolate or it is cooled and further processed into its two components – cocoa butter and cocoa solids (cocoa powder).

Bitter chocolate contains cocoa solids and cocoa butter in varying proportions, without any added sugar. Powdered baking cocoa, which contains more fibre than cocoa butter, can be processed to produce Dutch cocoa.

Much of the chocolate consumed today is in the form of sweet chocolate – a combination of cocoa solids, cocoa butter or added vegetable oils, and sugar. Milk chocolate is sweet chocolate that additionally contains milk powder or condensed milk. White chocolate contains cocoa butter, sugar and milk, but no cocoa solids.

Between 2016 and 2017, global cocoa prices dropped by more than a third. The number of farmers fell because the benefits were so poor that young people didn't want to stay in the profession. Farmers remained in poverty as their income failed to keep up with rising production costs and household expenses.

Farmers began to turn to illegal small-scale gold mining (galamsey). The practice of galamsey (derived from the phrase "gather them and sell" is a local Ghanian term which literally means illegal small-scale gold mining) offers quick money but pollutes water and introduces heavy metals into the soil. The cocoa crops became neglected.

Projects such as Cocoa Horizons help to empower cocoa farmers to shift their smallholder farms into profitable cocoa farms, motivate new generations to stay in cocoa farming, and nurture their ambition with the aim of making farmers financially independent so they can take care of their families.

The Cocoa Horizons Foundation was formally established on February 25, 2015 in Zurich, Switzerland and is supervised by the Swiss Federal Foundation Supervisory Authority. Its mission is to improve the livelihoods of cocoa farmers and their communities through the promotion of sustainable, entrepreneurial farming, improved productivity and community development.

There are calls for the EU to look at legislation, aligned with the United Nation's Guiding Principles on Business and Human Rights, as it is by far the largest importer and consumer of cocoa in the world. As an industry, we are trying to strengthen human rights, and environmental due diligence requirements of companies in the global cocoa supply chains.

Ultimately, this means that the price of chocolate will increase, but by paying a sustainability premium for our chocolate, we are investing in efforts to lift farmers out of poverty, eradicate child labour and be carbon positive by 2025.

Once I found out what it took to produce a bar of chocolate, I no longer looked at the premium ranges and thought 'this is expensive'. Instead I looked at the budget brands and wondered 'how (and why) can they sell it so cheap'?

Whiskey Sour

The oldest historical mention of a whiskey sour was published in a Wisconsin newspaper in 1870.

In 1962 the Universidad del Cuyo published a story citing the Peruvian newspaper El Comercio de Iquique, which indicated that Eliot Stubb created the Whisky Sour in 1872.

Ingredients	○ 4.5 cl (3 part) Bourbon Whiskey ○ 3 cl (2 parts) fresh lemon juice ○ 1.5cl (1 part) Gomme (sugar) syrup ○ Dash egg white (optional)
Preparation	Shake with ice. Strain into a chilled Old Fashioned glass, garnish and serve.

CHAPTER EIGHT

The Leap of Faith

It's an odd feeling not going in to work when you've been doing it for twenty years of your life, day in and day out. Heaving your lap top backwards and forwards every day onto a packed commuter train that rarely runs to time and you can't guarantee a seat does get a little tiring, but when you don't have to do it, that weight off your shoulders isn't necessarily lifted.

Once I'd waved everyone off to work and school I had the house to myself to do exactly what I wanted to do. But what was that, exactly? I felt a bit lost all of a sudden.

I had no one to tell me what to do. How great is that? Except now I had to tell myself what to do. Which was what?

Just how am I supposed to set up a chocolate business from home?

The first step was to register my business with the local authority. I discovered this needs to be done at least 28 days before opening, so this had to be my first job before I did anything else. It's free to register your business and registration can't be refused. It was easily done online at https://www.gov.uk/food-business-registration.

Once registered, I knew I was going to be inspected by our local authority. The local Environmental Health office will automatically make an initial appointment once a business is registered, to okay the premises as fit for purpose. The mere thought of this terrified the life out of me. Would I need to refit the kitchen, get stainless steel splashbacks, replace any of the fittings? It's a scary prospect but an essential step, so it was time to feel the fear and meet it head-on. With the appointment in the diary I set about cleaning the kitchen to within an inch of its life.

As it turned out, the kitchen was fine for purpose, as chocolate is a low-risk product. The Environmental Health team are not there to prevent you from setting up a food business. They're there to help you, so if there are hurdles between you and your business, they will offer support and advice to help you surmount those obstacles.

I've seen a number of food businesses frustrated at the initial visit for two main reasons. The first is that Environmental Health don't like a washing machine in the kitchen area. I'm lucky to have a utility room, so that wasn't an issue for me, but I know a number of others for whom this has been a stumbling block, or at the very least a point for consideration. If there's no alternative place to site your machine then you must not do laundry during food preparation for business purposes. You don't want the presence of your sweaty gym kit contaminating someone's birthday cake, or a sock falling into a batch of caramel.

A food-based business will also need a separate sink for hand washing. I had a sink in the utility room and a sink with a separate half sink in the kitchen, so this wasn't an issue for me, but had I just had the one sink in the kitchen I would have needed to install a separate hand-wash sink unit to avoid any cross contamination. I've had to throw away a bowl of fresh hot soapy water that was ready for dishwashing on more than one occasion because someone decided to wash their hands in it.

Environmental Health gave me a long list of things to consider, however, such as avoiding heavily scented products around melted chocolate, which includes the cleaning products I use, avoiding wearing perfume, and avoiding cooking smells during production hours. Limiting my business to during the day when everyone else is at work or school was going to avoid a lot of issues, but during holiday times there was going to be a completely different set of considerations I needed to think about.

The herb pots on the window sills had to go as they attract flies and the last thing I wanted was an insect landing in the chocolate tank. That also meant I couldn't work with the doors and windows open during the summer unless I installed fly screens and insect zappers.

It was recommended I contact Trading Standards for advice on labelling my chocolates. The information you need to include on food labels is dependent on where and how you are planning on selling your products. If you are selling your products at local markets and events, and even online via your own website, then the requirements are minimal. If you're planning on distributing via retail outlets, or other online platforms such as Amazon, then the requirements are very different and will include things like barcoding, nutritional information and the ever-changing ingredient requirements.

It's worth considering your medium-term plans as well as your initial steps at this point. There's no point paying for a large professional print run based on distributing locally if you ultimately want to retail your products. If you can't print your labels at home, then it's better to give the consumer too much information than to have to start again a few months down the line.

As with most new businesses, my early labels were a sheet of home-printed stickers that I put on each box and bag. We had an inkjet printer – the kind where the ink runs if it gets wet, which wasn't something I'd considered until the first time we exhibited at an outdoors event in the rain.

I was recommended to get my Level 2 Food Hygiene certificate, which I did as an online course (https://www.highspeedtraining.co.uk/food-hygiene/) and gave me a solid grounding in basic hygiene principles and how to run a safe food business. It was a straightforward course and took me an afternoon to complete.

My next task was to perform my Hazard Analysis and Critical Control Points (HACCP). It's a "systematic preventive approach to food safety from biological, chemical and physical hazards in production processes that can cause the finished product to be unsafe, and designs measures to reduce these risks to a safe level". In simple terms, I had to write down anything and everything that could possibly go wrong at each and every step of the day and how to mitigate any risks. The HACCP was something that took several days to complete. Firstly, I walked through my day in theory and wrote down everything I could think of, and once I was happy I'd thought of everything I did a sample production day, cross-checking with my list and adding to it.

The HACCP is a list I always have to hand as it constantly evolves with each new piece of equipment purchased and every variable for every situation – most of which you will never have thought of until they happen, but worth noting, even if they may never happen again.

I used the Safer Food, Better Business guidance online, but since then the Food Standards Agency have introduced MyHACCP, which is a free web tool that guides the user through the process of developing a food safety management system based on the HACCP principles. The MyHACCP tool produces a safety management system for a food business and will show how your business can identify and control any hazards that occur in the food you manufacture.

MyHACCP is aimed at small food manufacturing businesses in the UK (businesses with fifty or fewer employees). Access to the tool is not available to food businesses outside the UK.

The HACCP goes hand-in-hand with a daily checklist – what do I need to do to get the kitchen ready for purpose each day, and what do I need to do once I've finished production? Again, that's a constantly evolving list as situations change. Then there's the cleaning schedule – how often do I need to clean out the fridge, wipe out the storage cupboards, mop the floor and so-on.

After the initial Environmental Health assessment I was given a second appointment two months later for them to observe how I work. By that time I needed to have all my paperwork in order (HACCP, Daily Checklist, Cleaning Schedule and a list of the companies I purchase packaging, equipment and ingredients from) for them to check, and then they watched me whilst I worked. Following that visit I was given a hygiene rating, which arrived in the post a few days later with my window sticker – the same signs seen in cafés, restaurants and take-aways. The rating is based on what is seen on the day of inspection and rating is from 5 (hygiene standards are very good) down to 0 (urgent improvement is required), based on the food hygiene standards found at the time. I was thrilled and relieved to be given a level 5 rating from day one.

Environmental Health come back every three years to reassess the working methods. As a home-based business they are supposed to make an appointment but for a commercial premises they will usually turn up unannounced. However, I've only ever had unscheduled visits, which was a little frustrating, particularly on the most recent occasion when I was trying to hand roll five hundred salted caramels for a John Lewis order before I loaded up the van to go and set up for a show the following day. Time was at a premium and I was flustered. I attempted to get the Officer to come back when it was more convenient but he was having none of it. Fortunately my level 5 rating came through intact.

Obviously if you move premises, then you will need to inform Environmental Health of the change. This will also impact your HACCP, daily checklist and cleaning schedule, so it's not just a question of moving the equipment to its new home and immediately upscaling production. This applies to moving to an outbuilding, converting a garage, or just building an extension to the existing kitchen, as well as shipping out to commercial premises. If you have more than one site then each individual premises needs to be registered. There's a huge amount of useful information and advice on https://www.food.gov.uk/.

As a commercial venture I also needed to register the business with Companies House. I let our accountant handle this, so it was one less headache for me to worry about. You can, however, do this online at https://www.gov.uk/limited-company-formation/register-your-company where there is plenty of information to help you decide whether you need to set up a limited company and how to register your business. It costs £12 to register your business and then £13 every year thereafter to file your annual return, or confirmation statement.

Choctails Ltd became incorporated on May 4th 2012. We were good to go.

Peach Bellini

The Bellini was invented sometime between 1934 and 1948 by Giuseppe Cipriani, founder of Harry's Bar in Venice, Italy. He named the drink the Bellini because its unique pink colour reminded him of the toga of a saint in a painting by 15th-century Venetian artist Giovanni Bellini.

Ingredients	<ul><li>10cl Prosecco</li><li>5cl Fresh Peach Puree</li></ul>
Preparation	Pour peach puree into a chilled Champagne flute, add sparkling wine and stir gently. Traditionally a Bellini uses white peaches for the fruit.

CHAPTER NINE

Keeping the Faith

In recent years I've regularly seen a Facebook post which resounded with me:

> "Kylie Jenner releases a lip gloss, people rush to buy it.
>
> Beyoncé puts out a new perfume, people rush to buy it.
>
> Dre has new headphones, people rush to buy them.
>
> A famous athlete releases a new shoe and everyone rushes to buy them.
>
> In almost every case those products are not even the best in their respective market. You're just paying for a name.
>
> A friend or family member starts a home-based business so they can create a better

87

lifestyle for themselves and their family, and people rush to ridicule, are wary, sceptical, and hesitant to buy anything.

Why are we as a society so quick to support those we don't know – celebrities who let their names be used to sell more products (so they can profit more) – but we seem to find all the reasons in the world to not support someone we actually know and care about?"

A few days after my redundancy we were enjoying a pub lunch. I'd now got my head around becoming self-employed and stopped looking at recruitment sites. We bumped into a drinking buddy who wasn't normally to be found in our local, especially during a weekday lunchtime. He tended to stick to the pubs close to the train station as he arrived back in the village in the evening.

Coincidentally, he had also been made redundant, so was taking a few days to catch up with people at the top of the village that he hadn't seen for a while whilst he considered his options. I could barely contain myself as I told him my plan to set up the chocolate business. The excitement bubbled up in me. Just the act of telling someone my plans made it so much more real. I was actually going to be setting up a chocolate business right here, in this village, less than half a mile from where I was currently standing.

I couldn't have felt more deflated when his immediate reaction was negative. He pointed out that we were currently in recession. There was no place for a handmade chocolate business in the market. There are enough companies out there selling budget chocolate to the people who want to satisfy their cravings. Luxury chocolates weren't what the public was after. My idea simply wouldn't fly. He spent a good ten minutes telling my why I was doing the wrong thing.

If I'd listened to him, I wouldn't be where I am today.

Instead of letting his negativity put doubts into my head, I listened to the people who thought it was a great idea. The ones who said "Oh wow, that's really exciting!" and asked about the type of chocolates I was planning to make. There was the couple who's faces lit up when I told them what I was going to do and said "I knew it! As soon as you were made redundant We knew that's what you'd do!" There were the people who immediately knew of a possible retail outlet I could try to sell my products into. These were the reactions which gave me a lift and put me back on track.

I also listened to my inner voice – the one which told me that this was my passion; the same voice that kept reminding me of the corporate treadmill that I most definitely didn't want to get back onto.

I'd decided to give the business six to twelve months to see how it took off. If it failed to get off the ground at all, then I needed to either change my offering completely, or admit defeat. If it bubbled away but didn't show signs of doing anything spectacular, then we might need to run it as a part-time business alongside another career. If it took off well enough, then I was going to stick with it. Of course, that was the option I really wanted to take, so it was up to me to make a success out of cocktail chocolates.

It was time to take a deep breath and take my products into the big wide world.

"If you build it, they will come" may have worked for Kevin Costner in Field of Dreams, but I knew the real world was going to be somewhat different. Yes, I had a great product that I believed in, but I knew I wasn't yet poised for success. Was I even market ready? I needed to engage with customers and gather feedback and guidance. Although I'd initially made chocolates for us, I now needed to consider the wider audience and work out who I wanted to sell our products to. In short, just making a quantity of chocolate and hoping for the best wasn't going to give rise to a successful business.

I began with local farmers' markets, my first event being the Wivenhoe Farmers' Market on 16 June 2012. It had been a while since I'd done any kind of selling, and I was more than a little trepidatious, but the one thing I did remember was that people buy people, so I stuck my best grin on my face and started to talk chocolate.

Slowly but surely I built up a good local following. It takes a while for regulars to get to know you and your product, but once they do, and like what you're selling, they'll make sure they make a point of coming back to your stall. Before long, you'll find yourself at a local event with someone saying "I was hoping you'd be here because I need some chocolate," or "Are these the Wivenhoe chocolates I've been hearing so much about?"

I watched the other stall holders closely. The ones who stood up and were happy to chat and banter were always busier than those who just sat down and gave the passers-by a half smile. This wasn't a time for British reserve.

At the same time, we had a website ready to take online sales, so that anyone who was undecided about purchasing on the spot at an event had an option to purchase later. It was a mantra I kept chanting to myself "make sure they don't leave empty handed", even if all they took was a leaflet or business card with our web address on it.

My first web order came through on 22 June 2012. It was a close friend who wanted something special for a dinner party and I was so excited that he'd not only thought of us but that our website worked properly. Even though we'd tested the website ourselves and placed orders, cancelled orders and refunded orders, it was still a relief when that first real order popped in proving that everything worked the way it should. It was such a thrill to receive that first order. In fact, I still get a thrill today when an email order notification comes through. It's absolutely true that whenever you order from an artisan producer, someone does a happy dance.

A few of my friends were quick to place online orders which gave me a real boost. They'd all been happy to take the free chocolates I'd distributed over the years, but the fact that they were willing to pay for them made me realise they weren't just paying lip service. And then the first order from someone I didn't know came in. It was obvious from the address that they'd seen us at a recent show. All of a sudden I was nervous about sending my chocolates out. Will they arrive okay? Will they like them?

If I put a 'Fragile' sticker on the box will the sorting office see that as a licence to throw the box around or will they handle them carefully? All the things I hadn't thought to be worried about when dispatching to friends and family were now nagging at me. For days I dreaded the negative feedback email or phone call, which never came.

Delivery can be a troublesome thing when you're sending food items. If you're sending jams and chutneys there's a breakage risk. Cakes can turn up as a mass of crumbs or squashed beyond all recognition. Does it need to be kept cold? If so that's another dimension to your packaging solutions. If you keep it local then you can deliver by hand, but if you want to distribute nationally, or even internationally, then there are a lot of additional factors to consider.

We used Meridien Packaging for our boxes as they had a wide range of confectionery packaging and postal boxes with specific dimensions to fit each size of chocolate box. I came across them one afternoon whilst searching for confectionery packaging online. They were a good one-stop shop for pretty much all my packaging needs at that time.

Gradually we built up a solid online following and I got even more of an ego boost when the repeat web orders began to come in, with people ordering for a second and third time and in larger quantities. I'll occasionally add a thank you gift for those who order regularly, most often in the form of a money-off coupon for their next order to persuade them to keep coming back. I've also found a hand-written note can go a long way, telling them about a new product I'm developing, or a show that I'm going to be at that's in their locale.

When we rebranded and updated our website we made sure to include a subscription service so that people could sign up for a regular supply of chocolate. It's great to know that so many people want a box of Choctails every month, and it keeps me busy developing new products, which I love to do.

I often glance back over my turnover from day one and remind myself just how many people I've made happy with a little chocolate (or even a lot).

Of course there will be days when you find your motivation slipping. Working alone and from home can feel completely unprotected. You can't break off and have a chat at the coffee machine to pick yourself up, and there isn't the routine of regular meetings and reports to give the week some structure. It's easy to let the gremlins throng in your head. These are the days when you need to think about why you started this journey in the first place and consider what you would be doing as an alternative. Having got off the corporate treadmill, do you want to get back on, or would you rather keep following your dreams?

Mojito

Havana, Cuba, is the birthplace of the Mojito, although the exact origin is the subject of debate. One story traces the Mojito to a 16th century drink known as "El Draque" after Sir Francis Drake, following an epidemic of dysentery and scurvy on board his ships. The local South American Indians had remedies for various tropical illnesses, so a boarding party went ashore on Cuba and came back with ingredients for an effective medicine; aguardiente de caña (a crude form of rum made from sugar cane) mixed with lime, sugarcane juice, and mint.

Ingredients	o 4cl White Rum o 3cl Fresh Lime Juice o 6 Sprigs of Mint o 2tsp Sugar or 2cl Sugar Syrup o Soda Water
Preparation	Muddle mint leaves with sugar and lime juice. Add a splash of soda and fill a tall glass with cracked ice. Pour the rum and top with soda water. Garnish with a sprig of mint leaves and lemon slice.

CHAPTER TEN

The highs and lows of exhibiting

As I mentioned earlier, I began selling at local farmers' markets, my first event being the Wivenhoe Farmers' Market on 16 June 2012. I took £57:75 over the three hours – I'd set myself a target of £50:00, so I was reasonably happy – and with it being my first market the organisers waived my pitch fee. This may or may not happen for a new exhibitor. Treat it as a bonus if it does.

As a newbie at an established market, I had the advantage of the curiosity factor. The downside of an established market, however, is that some people will come in to purchase from a couple of specific stall holders and not give you a second glance. Give it time. They'll notice you before too long.

I resisted the temptation to sit down. It's something I refuse to do to this day, even if the show lasts all day for several days and even if my feet, back, legs, shoulders, are protesting at me. If you're standing up, people are much more likely to engage with you. It's also rare that I pick up my phone whilst I'm on the stand. Again, people are less likely to engage with someone intent on scrolling through social media. If you want to post a picture to social media platforms to let your followers know where you are, then do it first thing before customers come through the doors.

Make sure to respect your boundaries. You've been allocated a space, and you need to display your wares so that they fit that space whilst still leaving you room to get out from behind your stall when you need to. I remember at one market a girl arrived selling home furnishings and proceeded to block off the access to the toilets, take up most of the aisle space, and made it difficult for people to get to the adjacent fruit and veg stall. It didn't go down well.

One thing you must do at a market is engage with the other stallholders. If you're on your own, then knowing who's on the neighbouring stall is a must – you need someone to keep an eye on your cash box if you need a comfort break at the very least.

The other stall holders have been there longer than you have and know the market and its attendees better than you. Treat them with respect and they'll take you under their wing. By paying attention to what was going on around me I learned that other stallholders were given discounts, or offered a trade-off, so I followed suit. I realised they were more likely to purchase from me if I'd purchased from them, so it became the place where I obtained my weekend food supplies. They're then more likely to point their customers towards your stall. Conversations yielded other markets and events that might be of interest to me. I left my first market with a long list of dates and phone numbers. I'd also caught up on a lot of local gossip!

Within a couple of hours of my first Wivenhoe market I'd been told of farmers' markets in Brightlingsea, Rowhedge, Frinton and Colchester. Colchester turned out to be a no-go as they already had a chocolate seller on their books and didn't want to duplicate (some markets are quite strict on this, so it's worth doing your research before approaching the organisers), but with the others that meant I had three Saturdays and one Thursday each month dedicated to local markets. I'd also heard of numerous one-off events around the region, all of which I said yes to.

It's quite common for organisers to offer a discount for booking six or twelve months in one go, but be wary of block-booking markets you know nothing about. If you find after the first market that it's not right for your product, then you'll be miserable for the entire duration. I'd advise you to visit the market first, and spend some time observing footfall and visitor motivation (are they just coming along to have a quick browse and a chat or are they here to shop?). If they have a café, and most markets do, then grab a cuppa and spend some time people watching.

Over the next few months I discovered the highs and lows of selling chocolate. Having taken a pitch at a school summer fair, I made sure I had a few non-alcoholic products with me. The day was cold and drizzly, so I loaded the car up nice and early to avoid a last minute panic. The sun came out not long after, and as I set up the stall I discovered several bags of chocolate had melted in the back window of the hatchback whilst it sat on the driveway. The evening sun then streamed straight into my gazebo and I spent the entire duration of the fair trying to devise creative ways of finding some shade.

Two lessons learned: don't load up until the last minute, and always request a pitch out of direct sunshine when you book. At a town show a few weeks later I'd specifically requested a pitch in the shade. Unfortunately when I arrived, someone had pitched in my allocated space and refused to switch, with a "just use my spot" attitude. Yes, you've guessed it, I was in full sunshine. Much as I complained to the organisers, I was stuck with the alternate pitch for the afternoon and ended up with a lot unsaleable, inedible bags of spoiled chocolate.

Bear in mind that if you are selling at farmers' markets and events, then that's what you're going to be spending your weekends and evenings doing. You're going to need to be flexible and you'll find you have to fit your social life around your business, especially in the early days when you are trying to get your business off the ground.

I discovered there were several local organisers who had a portfolio of events, so having done one of their shows, I would be told about the rest. Multi-show bookings can often mean you get a discount as well. There are a lot of organisers who run a fantastic show, well-advertised and well attended and who look after their stallholders as much (if not more so) as they do the people coming through the door. Justine Paul, who runs Suffolk Market Events, is one of the best show organisers I know, so as soon as I found out an event was part of her portfolio, I got myself on the list. There are, equally, a lot of organisers who are completely disorganised, put the whole show together on a shoe-string in order to maximise their own profit, and don't seem to care. Make sure you know who's organising your event before you book.

Talk to other stallholders about their experience, yes, but make sure you're talking to people who have a similar offering to you. The stall selling curry sauce jars will have a very different experience to the one selling gourmet dog biscuits. I was very tempted to exhibit at Car Fest a few years ago, and I spoke to a chilli sauce seller who'd had a phenomenal show. The ginger beer seller had sold out before lunchtime on the final day. The girl who sold handmade chocolates, however, made a loss.

A tip I was given several years ago, is to ask the organisers how many portaloos they have booked for the event. It gives you a big clue as to how many people they are expecting through the gates.

Essentially though, you don't know how well a show will work for you unless you try it. I've taken a stall at a couple of Christmas Craft Fairs where I've made an absolute killing because I was offering something completely different to the plethora of jewellery and candle stalls. Conversely, a spirit show, where again I was the only confectioner, saw me making a loss because everyone who attended was only interested in the drinks (mostly the free samples).

The biggest issue I had with saying yes to everything in the early days, was that most of the shows I was attending didn't really suit my core brand. Agreeing to exhibit at a school fair meant that I wanted to offer something which appealed to the children. My core range of alcoholic truffles wasn't going to hit the spot, so I was making chocolate lollipops, novelty shapes and bags of mini chocolate bars. It was time-consuming and meant I was focussing more on novelty chocolates than the products I'd built my business around. Once we became more established Simon kept repeating the adage "If you're having to make products to fit the event then it's not the right event for you."

And in that vein, if someone asks for something that's not in your range, or that's a slight alteration of one of your products, then it's not a guarantee they will come back to purchase it if you do manage to create it for them. Stick to your guns. It's your product. Believe in it. After all, if you've gone to the trouble of making an Irish Cream truffle in milk chocolate instead of white because someone said they would buy it, what happens when they don't want it after all?

Since 2012, I've had pitches at a plethora of different shows and at various times of year. It's been a long process to whittle these down into a list of events that really suit my product. There's been a lot of trial and error but gradually patterns began to emerge. Initially I said yes to every food and craft festival going. If it worked for me the first time around, then I would go back.

Sloe Comfortable Screw

A screwdriver is a popular drink made with orange juice and vodka and dates back to the 1940s, supposedly invented by interned American fliers. The Sloe Comfortable Screw is a variation on the Screwdriver with the inclusion of Sloe Gin and Southern Comfort.

Ingredients	○ 5cl (1 part) Vodka ○ 10cl (2 parts) Orange Juice ○ 10cl (2 parts) Sloe Gin ○ 5cl (1 part) Southern Comfort
Preparation	Mix in a highball glass with ice. Garnish and serve.

CHAPTER ELEVEN

Finding the right event for your product

As my business grew, the types of events I exhibited at changed. The local farmers' markets were gradually replaced with bigger events and I was going further afield. I was working at least three weekends out of four during my second and third years in business. During November and December I was rarely at home – just long enough to pick up fresh stock and clean thermals before heading off to my next show.

After many years of attending outdoor events, and after multiple gazebo replacements I began to come to the conclusion that I shouldn't be exhibiting if I'm going to be outdoors with my own gazebo. This wasn't a decision I took lightly, and I whittled it down slowly before I gave gazebo events up completely. First, I stopped taking on new events if it required me to take my own gazebo. I also didn't re-book at shows that hadn't been a huge success, before starting to drop shows I'd become a regular at. I'd come to the conclusion that the weather is never right, whatever the conditions.

If it's a hot and sunny day then the weather is too hot for chocolate. I've arrived armed with ice packs to put under the table cloth and still I've suffered more than a significant amount of melted chocolates that are no longer saleable. I can also guarantee the sun is going to creep round at some point causing me the stress of finding the shade from that moment on. You can't put the side-walls up and close off your gazebo from the public.

If the weather's wet, there's a risk of rain damage to the gazebo, the stock, or both – I've experienced all three. Watching the rain puddle onto the gazebo roof and then picking your moment to tip the water off at a strategic pause in footfall is more preferable to the water bursting in to your stall and drenching you and your stock at an inopportune moment when the roof bar breaks under the strain. Sideways rain is guaranteed to get into every nook and cranny.

If the weather's windy, then at best I'm going to be spending all day hanging on to gazebo legs and wind bars to stop it flying away, and at worst, trying to repair a gazebo damaged or broken by a rogue gust of wind (Gorilla tape is an essential addition to your toolbox). Even if it's still, get the leg weights out immediately the gazebo is up, or you could find yourself planted sideways in next door's pitch. Wind has a habit of gusting even on the calmest of days.

If it's cold, then it's just a case of making sure you're wearing the right clothes, remembering that you won't be able to move very far very often to generate your own heat. Feet will get cold very quickly. Hands will get so cold that it's difficult to count change or operate the card reader. If it's really cold then the chocolate will start to bloom as soon as it warms up – try putting your chocolate bar in the fridge and then watch it come up to room temperature. The layer of condensation which forms on the chocolate will ruin the appearance and mouth feel. It's the same process if the weather's cold.

If it's a two-day event and you're allowed to leave your gazebo up overnight I can guarantee you'll have a sleepless night worrying about how everything will fare overnight, from weather conditions to wild animals to potential theft. If you have to pack up at the end of each day then you've got the additional stress and logistics of setting up and breaking down every day, added to the physical effort needed to put up and take down a gazebo at each end of the day. I got so adept at doing this on my own, that I now get confused with how it's done when someone offers me a hand.

I would arrive home exhausted, thankful that Simon was in the final stages of dinner prep and had a gin and tonic ready poured for me as I walked through the door.

By 2016 I'd decided that I'd had enough of gazebo events. That's not to say that a lot of food sellers don't do well at this kind of show. Preserves and chutneys do a roaring trade from people wanting something different to spread on the burger they've just purchased, for example. It's just not the right environment for chocolates (particularly high end chocolates), or other products that are weather sensitive, as any profit is in danger of being wiped out by ruined stock, or having to purchase a replacement gazebo.

The next types of event to get struck off my list were the ones in a marquee. This was an improvement on the gazebo for two reasons. One was that I didn't have the extra hassle of putting up and taking down a gazebo – very welcome when you're tired at the end of a long day. The second plus point was that it was much more sturdy, so rainy days weren't a problem and windy days, generally, were okay. There are exceptions, but that's some seriously high winds before the marquee will take off (as happened at the Suffolk Show a few years ago).

The hot summer days were an absolute no-no in a marquee, and unfortunately this is when the majority of these shows take place. The heat builds up so much that it becomes stifling, and if there's a cookery display in the tent as well, then it just gets hotter and hotter and the chocolates get softer and softer. It's the same for products such as cupcakes – buttercream doesn't fare well at all in hot weather.

The other factor to consider during the summer months is transportation. If the weather's exceptionally hot and you've got a long journey, how will your products fare? You might need to consider a refrigerated van or large cool boxes to store everything in.

Food festivals are very dependent on the product you are offering. Cake slices go down a storm – something the public can pick up and eat at the event, as do burgers, ice creams and drinks. Over the last few years I've seen a shift as the food festival has become more of a day out with live music and family activities. Hence if you're serving food-to-go you'll do a roaring trade. The Prosecco Van will have a constant queue and the ice cream servers won't get a chance to step away from the stall. It's now less of an opportunity to buy something unusual. Be prepared to sample and give out leaflets, but not necessarily sell out. Shift your own focus into using it as a PR exercise and point them towards the website. Even if you haven't had the best show you should see an upswing in online orders down the line.

I also found that taking my products further afield wasn't always a guaranteed success. If it's a food festival then people tend to like to shop local, or buy from someone with a connection to the region. An event such as a flower festival or garden festival can work well, but the food marquee is incidental to the reason the public are there, so be cautious and do your research. Essentially, will your target market be attending the event?

I've often considered having a summer offering and a winter offering. Our core brand does extremely well from September through to May, but only ticks along during the summer. I toyed with the idea of producing a range of alcoholic lollies, sorbets and ice creams on more than one occasion, but that in itself would require a completely new set of equipment to produce, store and serve. It's worth considering, however, having two separate arms to your business, or at least a summer and a winter range of products.

I began to think bigger. In 2013 I did my first London Chocolate Show at Olympia. The pitch fees seemed astronomical and I had accommodation and parking costs on top. How on earth was I going to cover all my costs when every other stall was selling chocolate? It was incredible to see that every single producer there had started with the same base product and yet developed something unique. Everyone through the doors came to shop. I covered my costs and more.

It wasn't until 2016 that I decided to exhibit at the BBC Good Food Show. If I thought the costs of exhibiting at Olympia were expensive they were nothing compared to the NEC, so it was a big leap of faith. However, if you don't try, you won't find out if it suits your product or not.

I've discovered that where my products sit best are at specialist food events such as chocolate shows and good food events. Yes, the pitch fees are much greater, but these are the events where people come to shop for high end gifts and treats. By adding in a few local events, I was managing to find the optimum balance and getting some of my weekends back.

Margarita

According to cocktail historian David Wondrich, the margarita is merely a popular Mexican and American drink, the Daisy (margarita is Spanish for "daisy"), remade with tequila instead of brandy, which became popular during Prohibition as people drifted over the border for alcohol.

There is an account from 1936 of Iowa newspaper editor James Graham finding such a cocktail in Tijuana, years before any of the other margarita "creation myths".

Ingredients	o 3.5cl Tequila o 2cl Cointreau o 1.5cl Lime Juice
Preparation	Pour all ingredients into a shaker with ice. Shake well and strain into a Margarita glass rimmed with salt.

CHAPTER ELEVEN

Sampling

If you sell a food product then it goes without saying that you will need to provide samples to the public. How you do this depends on the type of product you sell.

People won't purchase a luxury food item without knowing it tastes great, so take a deep breath and let them try what you have to offer. Whether you let them sample everything in your range or just a selection is entirely up to you. Personally, I will take a selection of samples, usually one flavour from each of my collections and often coinciding with my chocolate bar range.

Traders selling oils and dressings will often have a small dish of each variety on their stall with small cubes of bread to dip in. I've seen some sausage producers have a sample of every variety they have with them and some fudge sellers with samples of every flavour available. The downside of this approach is that a lot of people will come along to try everything you've put out and then move on. It creates a crowd and a buzz around your stall which will in turn bring more people to you, but if they're just sampling, then it's not going to be a profitable event. You need to work hard to turn those samplers into buyers.

I'm more than happy to give out samples provided people want to engage with me. As soon as they make eye contact I'll offer them a sample of chocolate. It gives me the opportunity to fully engage with them and talk to them about the brand, which in turn is more likely to result in sales.

You will get people just out hunting samples and they're often quite brazen in the 'do you have samples'? approach. I've even had people come into my stall to pick up the tray I put down behind me whilst I served a customer, and then hand it around the hungry crowd in the vicinity. They often feel that because they've paid an entrance fee they're entitled to eat the equivalent in free food.

Make sure you have budgeted for samples when working out the costs for a show or an exhibition. Bigger shows mean more samples. The BBC Good Food Show, for example, will require many more samples than a local food festival or a farmer's market.

A good rule of thumb is to budget around 10% of your projected takings on samples. I'll open a £5 chocolate bar to use for samples at a farmers' market where I take £50. At the Good Food Show, where takings run into four figures, I'm going to need twenty times that.

I've experimented with a wide range of sample types over the years and there are pros and cons to all of them. Our less-than-perfect chocolates make great samples, but these need to be cut into pieces which is time-consuming when you're on the stand. It's the same with our chocolate bar range; again, they need to be cut into small pieces whilst you're exhibiting, but using the bars which have bloomed, or broken as they were being de-moulded, is a cost-effective way of using them up. For a more upmarket event, such as in-store sampling, I've used mini bon-bon moulds to make smaller versions of some of our chocolates. The finished product is much more attractive, and less time consuming at the actual event, but it's more expensive to produce a bespoke sample and you need to factor in the extra production time. My favoured method is to use pre-bought mini truffle spheres and pipe in our truffle fillings. It's quicker than moulding the chocolates and I can make a wider variety. Yes, there is an additional cost attached, but it's a lot easier when you are at a show, much quicker to produce, and looks attractive.

If you are being stocked by a major retailer you will be asked to do some instore sampling. Yes, another dent in your bottom line, but it's good to be able to talk direct to the customers and will definitely increase shelf sales. Just be careful you don't get trapped into visiting too many of their stores, as all travel and accommodation costs are your responsibility.

Sampling doesn't just mean providing tasters for the public at an event. If you are looking to move into retail, then you will need to send samples to prospective buyers, and of course not all of those who sample will end up buying from you.

If you're targeting the big names, then make sure they know who you are before you send any samples through. Don't send anything through without that initial contact as they have no idea who you are. The buyers are inundated with people trying to get their products onto the shelves and you need to stand out if they're going to remember you. When I targeted the big name retailers we had already had several conversations before any of them asked for samples. We had established an interest in the brand before they even tried any of our range.

When it comes to the smaller retailer, I now charge for any samples and then discount some or all of the cost from the price of their first invoice. Whether I charge them the retail or wholesale price for the samples depends a lot on how much they're asking for and how genuine I think they are.

I once received a request for a volume of samples which seemed excessive at the time, but it was for a company who said they supplied companies such as Waitrose and other high street retailers with hampers, so were looking for new products to include in their selections. They had a glossy website and it sounded like an exciting opportunity. I never heard back from them. Emails went unanswered, phone calls went straight to voicemail and the voicemails also went unanswered. When I checked back a few weeks later the website didn't exist any longer. I'd given someone £100 of my chocolate for nothing. From that moment on I started charging for my samples.

Every year, almost every chocolatier I know receives an email from someone who is opening a new tea shop and looking to spend at least £1,000 per month on chocolates and would like samples of our full range of chocolates. It's a classic way of people getting their Christmas chocolates for free, so be wary.

The genuine companies will be more than happy to pay for the samples. The not-so-genuine won't. I've had one potential retailer pay up front for a sample set and then complain that they had bloomed so needed a refund.

As well as samples, I also get asked for a lot of raffle prizes and with that kind of request I use my discretion. If it's a charity close to my heart then I'll send them a box of chocolates but it's impossible to say yes to every request. I had over a hundred requests one year. That's a lot of chocolate to give away if I'd supported everyone.

Similarly, I get inundated with requests to include my products in goody bags. When these people contact you asking for free samples they usually assume you have included them in your budget, if they assume anything at all. These kind of free hand outs are generally for the big name brands and have little or no impact for the independent food producer.

Unless you are supplying a national supermarket chain or major high street retailer, your goody bag product will be eaten and forgotten about. The whole point of a "free" sample is that the person who consumes it sees it on the shelves the next time they go shopping. I have occasionally found it a useful way of getting through Christmas overstocks before they go out of date, but it rarely leads to more than a couple of online sales. At best, you can expect a small buzz on social media for a couple of days.

And then there's the ultimate 'if you send me some of your products I'll give you exposure on social media in return'. That is not going to put money in your cash box. You've just opened the floodgates for vloggers and bloggers to ask you for the same. So what if they can increase your following? Having the most followers and likes is not the answer to increasing sales.

Woo Woo

A quaffable vodka-based cocktail from the 1980s.

Ingredients	o 2 parts (1oz) Vodka o 1 part (5oz) Peach Schnapps o 4 parts (2 oz) Cranberry Juice
Preparation	Build all ingredients in a highball glass filled with ice. Garnish with a lime wedge .

CHAPTER TWELVE

Time Management

Following my first Wivenhoe farmer's market I got to know more and more local producers and was introduced to a number of events that I wouldn't have heard about otherwise. Not knowing which events would be right for me, I said yes to everything. Pitch fees were handed over and I put together an A4 folder containing all the event details organised in chronological order. It was only at that point that I realised December was packed with events almost every day and I'd failed to factor in the time to make the chocolates.

Time management is hugely important when you're self-employed. On a day-to-day basis you have to make the best use of the hours you have available during the day. If you're a food producer with a family, you have to make sure that your production doesn't interfere with meal time routines. For me, as soon as the children had finished breakfast I would prep the kitchen so that I was ready to start production the second they left the house. I would then make sure I'd finished by the time they arrived home and use the first hour after they got back to do my washing up and cleaning down. After that I would do my admin. Yes, the internet connection was slower once they were home, but it was a better use of my time than trying to make chocolate around post-school snacks and washing PE kits.

A product such as chocolate will take on scents and aromas from the atmosphere when it's in liquid form, so teenage girls with a penchant for marinating in perfume are not a good combination. Neither are cooking aromas, so if it's curry for dinner don't have it bubbling away in the slow cooker all day. I once made a batch of salted caramel samples and left the chocolate room door open whilst I prepared a fish supper. When I quality tested the finished batch the caramels had a fishy undertone and so couldn't be used. All of these occurrences went into my HACCP document and had to be mitigated for.

By the time I started Choctails, Simon's children were in their teens and becoming more independent. As they got older a lot of things became easier. I filled the freezer with home-made ping dinners for them, so now all I had to make sure of was that I wasn't needing the microwave when they wanted to eat, meaning I could extend my production time if necessary. They agreed to take responsibility for their own laundry, which meant I didn't need to keep on top of which PE kit was needed urgently, or if they had a clean shirt for the next day.

School holidays with teenagers can be a little challenging. Between us we'd agreed on a meal schedule so that I would stop production between certain hours to allow them access to the kitchen to make meals. It was great in theory. In reality, I had a teenager who slept until 3pm and then wandered into the kitchen wanting to make beans on toast whilst I was in the middle of microwaving the chocolate for the truffle fillings. Now I have to stop work and wait for him to prepare his meal (breakfast? lunch?) and then fully clean and deodorise the microwave before I can pick up again. A tip I discovered some months later was that microwaving a disinfectant wipe for a few seconds will remove any lingering odours.

I would grab hold of every opportunity for extra production time. There were a number of afternoons when both children were at after-school activities, giving me an extra hour. There were the occasional evenings when everyone was out of the house, giving me at least another two hours. However, life constantly throws you a curve ball. There's the phone call when the late bus hasn't turned up, and they've spent the emergency bus fare you told them to keep safe for just such a scenario. Now you need to stop what you're doing and go to collect them. There's the phone call ten minutes after they've said they'll go somewhere by bike to let you know they've picked up another puncture and need that lift after all. Expect the unexpected at all times.

As a general rule of thumb I tried to keep production days to Monday through to Thursday, leaving Friday for packing, wrapping and planning but leaving me an extra week day available if I was up against it and needed the additional production time.

Hand in hand with effective time management is motivation. I discovered that if I'm really not in the mood for chocolate making, the day could start to slip away with procrastination, and before I knew it my seven available hours were whittled away to nothing. That's not a problem if you've given yourself a long lead time, but if you've got production deadlines you just can't afford to take that kind of laid-back attitude towards your business.

Luckily I'd had it drilled into me from an early age that 'you can waste time with your friends once your chores are done' and I was seeing the sense in that approach when it came to running my own business. Plus, I was doing something I really loved, so it didn't feel like work. Except that it's no longer a hobby to pick up when you want to, and that can put an entirely different perspective on everything.

Yes, I've had my share of days when I really didn't want to make chocolate and if the work load is light and I know I can catch up relatively easily then I'll allow myself the time away to recharge. Yes, you will have days when it all feels like things are getting on top of you, especially with a home-based business where you can never get away from it all, and that's perfectly normal. I have various ways of dealing with this kind of slump, depending on how bad the slump feels and depending on the workload.

Some mornings I can wake up feeling lethargic with an 'I can't be bothered' attitude but knowing I've got a production target to achieve. That's when I stick on my running shoes and pound the pavements for an hour. By the time I've got back I feel energised and ready to tackle whatever I need to, and I know my subsequent increased productivity more than makes up for that hour that I was worried about losing. I also find that my subconscious sorts out a lot of detail for me whilst I'm running, so by the time I get back my schedule has been planned and I can get straight to it.

It could be that you're just hankering after some face-to-face interaction, and networking groups can be a perfect antidote to this. You get to mix with other business owners to discuss common issues and solutions, and it can be a good way to generate more business. It's a bit of time away from your 'office' each week and can help you regain a sense of perspective. I've made some great friends as well as generating new business this way.

If production allows, then take the day off. You're the boss. It's allowed. Go and have lunch with a friend. Read a book. Whatever. But if you really feel that you need the time away, and your diary allows, then take it. I've also found that on days like this if I 'force' myself to produce chocolate the results are never great and I end up with more than normal wastage, so I've not really gained much by the end of the working day.

Some days I just need a stern talking to. I'll ask myself 'what do I want to be doing instead?' Usually, I can't come up with a sensible answer to that one, so it's a case of just getting stuck in and what do you know, it turns out that's what I wanted to be doing all along!

It might be that I rearrange my week so that I'm doing admin on a day I was planning on being in production and vice-versa. Don't be afraid to adapt your schedule to suit your mood. Whilst planning is important, so is flexibility.

Another thing I'll think about is what I'd been planning to achieve that day and then visualise the scenario where I take the day off versus the one where I carried on regardless. The thought of having nothing more to show tomorrow is usually enough to have me scurrying back to the kitchen.

Targets and goals are hugely important. Obviously sales goals are key, but there are goals at every step of the production process. How many chocolates do I need to make this month, week, day? How many extra trays do I need to factor in to cover wastage and allow me additional chocolates to quality test each batch?

Make sure your targets are achievable though. Yes, stretch yourself, but if you're getting further and further behind each day, then you need to be more realistic with your planning. I've regularly been a victim to the 'everything takes longer than you think' axiom. Allow yourself more time than you think you're going to need. Of course, there are days when that's not possible and you've got to work late but that's all part of the fun. Yes, it might hurt your social life for a short while, but when you've delivered that big order you'll have the most amazing sense of achievement, and by heck you'll have earned a serious night out!

I'm a big fan of a 'to do' list. I like to see my long list being whittled down over the course of the week. If it's written down, it's tangible and it can't be forgotten. It's easy to overlook something if it's kept in your head. To that end I have a pad of flip chart paper hanging on one of my doors so that I can see what I need to do and have the satisfaction of crossing each thing off as I complete it.

I'm the sort of person who prefers a tangible planner to an electronic one. If it's in hard copy I find it easier to keep track of everything. Once I'd realised the crazy first December I'd set myself, I put together an excel spreadsheet, which rapidly turned into a Gantt chart (a type of bar chart that illustrates a project schedule), helping me to plan production and event logistics. I've kept a production planner ever since then, and it really helps.

I'm lucky in the respect that my chocolates don't contain cream or eggs which shorten the shelf life. Alcohol acts as a preservative, so although I hadn't got a definitive shelf life in my early days, I knew I was getting at least a month from my chocolates. That did at least take some of the pressure off from the production schedule.

If you make chocolates using fresh cream, then your shelf life will be around two weeks. That means your product needs to be made as last minute as possible. Similarly, if you're a celebration cake expert, you want everything to be as fresh as possible. Gone are the days of the fruit cake that can be made months in advance. A red velvet cake or a vanilla sponge will need to be made the day before and iced just in time. If that's your business, then you have to be prepared to pull an all-nighter before the client's party and accept that you'll be fuelled on sugar and caffeine until it's been safely delivered.

If you're a brownie producer, then yes, you will inevitably need to make fresh stock for an event, but these are the kind of products that can be successfully frozen, which can help when you've got a lot of events in a short space of time.

Everything comes down to preparation and planning. It may take a little trial and error to work out how much stock you need to make in advance before an exhibition or event, but do some research and work out a realistic volume of stock to take with you. Being ambitious is good, but think about what you're going to do with any stock left over as part of your event plan.

I now have a multiple-planner system. We have a year planner to detail holiday dates and both personal and Choctails' events so that we can see at a glance if a date is free or not. I also have a monthly wall calendar which goes into more detail on the top level events and includes meetings and appointments. The monthly calendar then feeds into a weekly planner which lists my 'to-do' items and a daily schedule broken into half-hourly slots so that I can micro-plan my day. The weekly / daily planner has now evolved into a magnetic white-board. I use magnetic colour-coded strips I can write on and wipe clean to move things around as necessary. I tried having a series of A5 files with date dividers, but that didn't work for me as I had to remember to look ahead. Seeing it on a calendar or planner every time I walk past keeps things in my head.

The trick is to find a system that works best for you. If you're happier having everything in electronic format, with reminder notifications, then use that, but do remember to have a back-up in case your device fails.

Singapore Sling

This long drink was developed sometime before 1915 by Ngiam Tong Boon, a bartender working at the Long Bar in Raffles Hotel, Singapore. It was initially called the Gin Sling.

A sling was originally a North American drink composed of spirit and water, sweetened and flavoured.

Ingredients	<ul><li>3cl Gin</li><li>1.5cl Cherry Brandy</li><li>0.75cl Cointreau</li><li>0.75cl DOM Benedictine</li><li>1cl Grenadine</li><li>12cl Pineapple Juice</li><li>1.5cl Fresh Lime Juice</li><li>1 dash Angostura Bitters</li></ul>
Preparation	Pour all ingredients into a cocktail shaker filled with ice cubes. Shake well. Strain into a highball glass. Garnish with pineapple and a cocktail cherry.

CHAPTER THIRTEEN

Storage and Shelf Life

I'm the kind of girl who has a chocolate room in her house. Sounds great, doesn't it? It certainly smells great! What was once our dining room had now become a place to store chocolate.

We're lucky to have a kitchen which is big enough to hold a dining table, and the majority of our meals have always been eaten in there, so the loss of the dining room was only a minor inconvenience. The size and layout of the kitchen allows me a production space which doesn't get in the way of making teas, coffees and snacks. In those early days I could also store all my moulds and equipment in a space in the utility room after I'd finished work.

The made chocolates needed a dedicated space and so we turned the dining room over to chocolate storage. It's a north-facing room, so gets no direct sunlight and is generally cool. It's not a room we make a huge amount of use of – visitors and special occasions, in the main. The beautiful sturdy dining table we bought seven years ago when we decorated, has rarely seen the light of day, although I do make an effort to clear everything away over Christmas and New Year and other special occasions.

As Choctails grew bigger, storage became more of a problem. I needed more and more moulds to cope with bigger volumes, and an additional melting tank, or two. I needed to keep more ingredients in stock, particularly at key times of year.

Our next step was to install a large shelving unit in the garage. Who uses their garage for cars these days anyway? Now I had somewhere to keep the growing number of containers full of chocolate moulds and organise them properly as well as somewhere to store postal packaging boxes and exhibition paraphernalia. We couldn't use the garage for food storage due to the fact that we occasionally get mice hibernating in there, and that also meant the boxes for the moulds and packaging needed to be airtight. There are plenty of storage solutions available, but if you're making food products then airtight containers are an absolute must.

Storing the moulds in the garage, however, meant that I needed to keep on top of my production plan and make sure the moulds I was going to be using each day had been brought in to the kitchen early enough in the winter months to get them up to room temperature.

Storing half-made chocolates was also becoming challenging. Once the moulds have been coated with chocolate and the fillings piped in, they need twenty four hours to set before capping off with another layer of chocolate. That meant I needed to store the trays overnight somewhere away from food preparation. I mentioned earlier the salted caramels with the fishy undertones, which was a direct result of food aromas permeating the half-made product.

Initially the dining table was a perfect place to leave the trays (provided I kept the door shut!) but eventually there wasn't enough space on there. Placing moulds on top of each other meant the bottom trays hadn't been exposed to the air and so weren't fully set. My next essential piece of equipment was a racking trolley which I wheeled into the kitchen every morning and back into the dining room every evening. The chocolate trays could be left on the trolley overnight to set and the storage footprint was a lot smaller. The sound of the trolley being wheeled out of the kitchen was almost like a dinner gong, signalling that meal preparation could begin again. It made things much easier to manage and the risk of dropping a chocolate tray as I walked between the two rooms was now eliminated.

The finished chocolates were all stored in the dining room. We had boxes for each different variety of individual truffle. We had some ready-packed gift boxes. We had bags of chocolates. We had chocolate bars. Everything had its space and place depending on where in the production and sales chain it was at that moment in time. Again, we had a variety of storage boxes to accommodate the ever-growing volumes of chocolate appearing.

As we've grown bigger and need to be more accountable at each step of the process, storage solutions have developed. Each box for the loose chocolates now has a wipe-clean panel on the front where we can note production dates and quantities. As Christmas approaches we have two boxes for each variety instead of one, as well as a larger stock of pre-prepared collections we can pick off the shelf as the orders come in. Everything is logged and coded, so if there are any complaints we know which batch the chocolates came from and can investigate any issues.

My kitchen space has evolved as well. Initially I was using a space by the hob. Now I have a marble slab which has storage underneath for all my equipment and some of the ingredients such as flavouring oils.

One extra dimension we needed was to know what our shelf lives were. Initially it wasn't something we had properly tested. Our early batches had lasted pretty well over a few weeks, but we had no idea, other than the fact that they'd all seemed okay when we ate them, and we never managed to keep them more than a couple of months. So now I needed an additional space to test the life of each chocolate variety.

My initial shelf life study was simply a case of storing twelve of each variety and keeping them cool and dry, and then tasting one each month. We worked on the principle that whilst most of our chocolates were fine at the end of twelve months, there were a significant number that started to lose character at around the seven to eight month mark, so we gave our chocolates a six month shelf life from date of production.

I've maintained a corner in the chocolate room which holds a separate stack of boxes containing chocolates at various ages, currently in testing. If we change an ingredient in one of our standard range of chocolates then we need to test again, noting down any visual and flavour changes over its lifespan and using the previous iteration as a control batch. All new products have gone through a twelve month cycle before we release them on the public.

Our testing processes are now a little more vigorous than just eating a chocolate each month, and needed to be more robust once we started supplying big name retailers. We need to take images of the cut chocolates each month to monitor any visual changes, check for crystallisation or deterioration, and then monitor factors such as pH levels. We also keep a selection from every batch currently in distribution until the best before date has passed, just in case we need to investigate any feedback.

There are companies who will test shelf life for you and if you are working towards BRC (British Retail Consortium) or SALSA (Safe And Local Supplier Approval) Accreditation, you will need shelf-life verification reports to demonstrate that you meet the audit standard requirements. They can determine the shelf life of your product using real-time and accelerated techniques. Your local Environmental Health team will be able to offer advice on the best route for your product.

Over the years we've thought about taking a unit or retail premises, so that we can have our house back, but the costs are quite prohibitive. I also like the convenience of working at home – the commute is definitely easier! The downside is that you never get away from it. Most days, I really don't mind that at all – do something you love and you'll never have to work another day in your life, after all – but there are days when I really wish I could make myself take a break. It's just too tempting to keep working at it whenever I have spare time at the weekends or in the evening, and that makes it more difficult to take a break. My ideal set-up would be a smaller house with an outbuilding, so that the business is on my doorstep but I can close the door on it at the end of the working day and switch off.

As well as storing equipment, products and ingredients, there are all the additional items such as packaging, paperwork, recipe books, sales materials, exhibition paraphernalia, to think about. As your business grows you'll have additional accoutrements to find a space for. Slowly but surely, as the business has grown and the family has grown up and moved out, Choctails has taken over every spare space in the house.

Pina Colada

The earliest known story of the Pina Colada states that in the 19th century a Puerto Rican pirate gave his crew a cocktail that contained coconut, pineapple and white rum to boost their morale.

Ingredients	o 3cl White Rum o 9cl Pineapple Juice o 3cl Cream of Coconut
Preparation	Blend all the ingredients with ice in an electric blender and pour into a large goblet or Poco Grande glass.

CHAPTER FOURTEEN

Branding

My initial idea for the Choctails brand was something simple, elegant and understated. At the local markets and events the feedback was great and people loved the simplicity of our packaging. We'd gone for the simple elegance of having our logo foil-blocked onto some off-the-shelf packaging. It's a popular, cost-effective solution used by a lot of food companies, particularly confectioners.

Our first foray into retail, however, made us realise our current packaging solution wasn't going to translate to an on-the-shelf product. It says 'Choctails' on the box, but what's inside? We knew, but no-one else did and that could lead to potential customers opening the box. Not very hygienic when they drop all the chocolates onto the shop floor!

I looked at having a mix of clear-lidded boxes alongside the solid box tops which was okay, but still wasn't appealing. The product inside was great, but how did we put that across to a customer if they didn't have time to stop and chat and sample?

Call it naivety, call it arrogance, but it's a trap a lot of us fall into. If I'd had a purple box with the word 'Cadbury' stamped on the front, people would immediately identify with the brand, but we were far from being that kind of household name.

Your brand identity is something that becomes more important the bigger your business becomes. If your intention is to stay local and market yourself at shows and markets, then you don't necessarily need anything flashy. An eye-catching hand-painted banner and home-printed labels is enough to get you started. However, if you're not there to talk to people about what you're selling then your packaging needs to tell the customer everything they need to know, and quickly.

I'd taken a stand at the Speciality and Fine Food Fair at Olympia in September 2013 – a huge trade show for the food and drink industry – and had a lot of interest in my product but nothing concrete. What I did find, however, was my Branding Agency.

My first reaction when someone asked if they could talk to me about my brand was 'what's wrong with my brand?' The man who'd asked the question seemed personable and self-assured. After a brief conversation he took my business card and I was determined that that was the end of that.

When he called back a few days later, however, I decided I had nothing to lose by having a conversation with them – I could always say no and walk away if I wasn't happy.

Coker Brand Design have an impressive portfolio and an enthusiasm for working with small businesses and start-ups. From the outset it felt like a collaboration. Simon and Jenny Coker spent several hours talking to me about my business right from its inception, getting an understanding of how we operated, what we stood for, and where we wanted to be. We also talked about my own personal likes and dislikes and the kind of brands which spoke to me.

There were a number of concepts they put forward to us, but the one we kept going back to was the 'swirls' design. Initially it was a close run thing between that and a design which reminded me of the Jack Daniels brand, but having stuck the concept designs on the wall and lived with them for the best part of two weeks, the swirls was the one which always caught our eye.

Once we had a basic concept they began to build on that. I've always loved Art Deco and the way it combines geometric design with the exotic. With it being a pastiche of many different, sometimes contradictory, styles, there's an element of rebelliousness as well as luxury, glamour and exuberance – I am, after all, the kind of girl who'll wear Converse with a ball gown because they're much more practical and comfortable than a pair of car-to-bar heels.

Coker's designs put a modern twist on the classic Art Deco style and captured all of those elements. It fitted the

Choctails concept as well as summing me up. When they came up with the 'Cocktail Obsessed Chocolatier' tag line, I was completely won over. I had my own identity. Choctails had its own identity.

Next came the hard work for us. We had to decide how to package our chocolates into collections. At the time I had every size of chocolate box that Meridien Packaging supplied (2, 4, 6, 8, 12, 16, 24, 48). We had bags of individual flavours. We had novelty chocolate shapes. As people had come along and asked for something specific that we didn't already stock, I'd gone away and made it, thinking it was an essential addition to the range. In short, I was trying to be all things to all people.

It was time to pare everything back to basics. I knew I wanted a box which held one of each of our flavours but beyond that I was at a bit of a loss. I was also thinking about redeveloping some of the collection. It was time to get the Long Island Iced Tea, amongst others, into the range, and this was a perfect opportunity to bring in some new varieties.

I'd come home from a show one weekend to find Simon preparing dinner with a knowing smile on his face and a piece of paper next to my ready-poured Gin & Tonic. He'd printed out our list of chocolates and at the top of the page was written:

- Classic Cocktails
- Aperitif Cocktails
- After Dinner Cocktails

He'd also made a start on categorising the individual flavours. It was so simple and so obvious a solution that I was a little jealous I hadn't thought of it myself. In short, he'd cracked it.

We decided to go with 12-chocolate collections as that was the size of box which had historically sold the most, and now it was over to me to develop the flavours to go into those collections. Our current range had some quirky-named truffles but they weren't a recognised cocktail, so they were dropped or adapted. The Galliano truffle was out. The Tequila and Lime truffle quickly became a Margarita. The Sloe Comfortable Screw I'd been developing was now added to the collection. I also changed some of the mould designs I was using.

A rebrand is a perfect opportunity to work out where you want to take your business next and get it ready for that next step. We wanted to get into retailing and this gave us the next-level product to be able to do that.

One thing we also needed to consider were our price points and this is where things become more tricky. Where did we want the business to go, ultimately? In essence, there were two routes to consider.

The first retail option was supplying local independent shops such as farm shops and delis. With this option you can see how your brand is received. You'll get feedback on how sales are going each week, month, year. Production costs are fairly high as everything is done by hand with little or no automation. Your product is high quality, usually using premium ingredients, and your distribution is small-scale with orders usually delivered in person. With this route you develop a relationship with your independent retailer and adjust order volumes as and when required. This is a classic low-volume-high-margin approach. As a small operation we knew we could make a decent profit.

The second retail route is specifically aimed at supplying bigger stores from day one. If being stocked in supermarkets or large retailers is your goal from the start, then you need to focus all your numbers on high volume. You need to factor in all the associated costs and have your distribution ready to go as soon as it's needed.

We were intent on growing organically, and I knew we weren't in a position to be stocked in supermarkets, so we took the first route option and based our price points on that.

One thing I would advise to avoid is a sale-or-return policy. Against my better judgement I was persuaded to do this for a deli that was just starting up and we were trying to help each other out. What happened was that once the first drop went out of date I was asked to replace any products left with fresh stock. Although there wasn't a huge volume left, it meant that I was landed with a significant quantity of out of date chocolates that I couldn't do anything with. I'd essentially made a 50 mile round trip to collect something that needed to go into the bin.

When working out costs, packaging will be by far your biggest outlay. It's just the way things are. Yes, you can shop around, but ultimately this is where the bulk of your costs will lie. A box of chocolates obviously comes in a box, so there's the cost of the box itself, but it's more than just buying a quantity of boxes.

With a bespoke box you will have the cost of printing and assembly. I found a company who would print a large run for me to make things more cost-effective, and then I could call off the boxes in a manageable volume. On top of that you may or may not have a shipping cost. If you don't, then it's likely that the cost of delivering your consignment will have been incorporated into the overall cost of the boxes, so take that into account when you're getting packaging quotes. Add on to the cost of the box the cost of the cutter guides. This is a one-off purchase, so the more boxes you have printed the less it will have an impact, but it's an initial outlay that needs to be considered, along with things like artwork.

I can't send my chocolates out rattling around in a cardboard box, so I need some kind of insert. I use a plastic vac-formed tray or a card divider. With card you'll need to put your chocolates into petits fours cups, otherwise they start taking on the flavour of cardboard. If you're using vac-formed trays then make sure that the dimensions are right for your box. I've found a cheaper alternative along the way, only to discover that the tray didn't quite fit the box and some of the chocolates were too large for the holes.

A more established brand might elect to have a bespoke insert tray created. This makes the contents look far more special and have a much bigger impact when the box is opened. However, this will increase the packaging costs and if you have multiple lines you will need multiple designs.

Once the chocolates are in the tray, we place a cushion pad on top to protect the chocolates from falling out, and also from taking on the flavour of the cardboard lid. We then wrap a sheet of tissue paper around for extra security and seal with a Choctails sticker (another cutter guide and set-up costs on top of printing and artwork costs). The menu card goes on top of that (yet another cutter guide and more printing and artwork costs). The whole thing is then wrapped in clear film to give it a security seal and make it airtight. So having worked out the cost of the box I then have to add vac-forme, cushion pad, tissue paper, sticker, menu card, film wrap. On top of all of those costs are the small but significant extras like Sellotape, date stickers, batch stickers.

As chocolates are an indulgence we knew we needed some theatre to opening the box, hence the extras such as tissue paper and branded stickers. Yes, we could have reduced this kind of cost, but it would also have removed the glamour and the impact. We wanted the brand experience to have as much impact as the chocolates themselves.

With packaging, another factor that is becoming increasingly important is eco-friendly and recyclable packaging. Whilst consumers aren't yet demanding it, the chances are they will before long, so if you're about to start your journey, this is something you really do need to consider. We are moving away from the plastic vac-formed trays in favour of card inserts, for example, and are looking for an alternative to the non-recyclable film wrapping.

Branding is more than just having a name and a tag line and some pretty packaging. It's the whole experience. We do our utmost to make every touch point a positive brand experience, be it the way I drive and park the van, navigate the public as I build up and break down the stand, interact directly with customers, or deal with an online order.

Of course, it wasn't just the chocolates which had a makeover. We needed new branded clothing and exhibition paraphernalia. Our trusty Ford Transit Connect needed a new paint job. It's very easy to get carried away. My advice would be to focus on the essentials and gradually replace or update the not-so-key items over time.

Our new branding certainly had an impact. Our first show was the Brighton Chocolate Festival in March 2014 and the black and white swirls definitely drew the eye. I was ecstatic with the work we had all put in and the public were extremely complimentary.

Hurricane

The creation of the passion fruit-coloured relative of the daiquiri is credited to New Orleans tavern owner Pat O'Brien. The bar allegedly started as a speakeasy called Mr O'Brien's Club Tipperary and the password was "storm's brewin'"

Ingredients	○ One part dark rum ○ One part white rum ○ Half part over-proofed rum ○ Passion fruit syrup ○ Lemon juice
Preparation	Shake ingredients with ice, then pour into a hurricane lamp-shaped glass and serve over ice.

CHAPTER FIFTEEN

Social Media, and Marketing

When I set up Choctails in 2012 social media wasn't as important as it is now, so I've only gradually adopted various platforms. I set up a Facebook page for Choctails on day one, but it was a while before I set up a Twitter account. Instagram hadn't yet been launched, but I was advised to do that in late 2014 by a social media and marketing expert, as my product is quite visual.

Social media is one of the best ways to get your name into the public domain. It's a great way to boost your brand and connect with your target audience on a more personal level.

In the early days you'll want to take control of all your own social media and marketing in order to keep the costs down, so take some time to research your platforms and have a plan.

Whilst you want to get your message out to as many people as possible, avoid falling into the trap of getting as many followers as you can. Quantity does not equal quality on social media. Focus instead on getting quality followers who will engage with you, share your posts and news, and ultimately purchase from you.

Facebook is one of the most popular platforms for personal and business use. Make sure you publicise your page and post a link to it anywhere you can, including having a Facebook icon on your website. Once you've created a strong following make sure you post status updates and photos to share your products, offers and services. Post content that gets your audience to engage with your posts. The more people engage, the more you'll appear in others' timelines.

Most people use Facebook as a personal network to connect with friends and family, so make sure you fit into this atmosphere naturally. Don't make it solely about selling. Make use of features such as polls from time to time. It's a way of getting some audience interaction and it doesn't always have to be a serious business-related

163

poll. Ask questions and try to get people involved in a conversation with you. They're more likely to remember you when they need what you're offering.

I use Facebook to highlight shows and events that we're at and drop in the occasional product-related post, such as new product launches and special offers. Alongside that, I'll put some themed content in, such as recipes for a Monday Mocktail, a Cocktail of the Week for Friday afternoon, hot chocolate recipes in the autumn and so-on. I drop in the odd post about what we're up to, such as mixing cocktails on National Cocktail Day, or the cheesecake we're enjoying on National Cheesecake Day. Hashtags don't have as much gravitas on Facebook as they do on other social media platforms, so don't go crazy with them, or better still, avoid them altogether.

With Facebook, use the Insights section on your business page to work out the best times of day to post about you and your brand. You can see the key times of day when your audience is online and you can time your posts to coincide with that. Make it personal so that they get to know you as well as your product and avoid a constant barrage of sales posts.

Facebook is also a great place to network. Have a look around for networks that are relevant to you, your business, and your local community and join the conversation. I'm a member of the Food Hub, which is a source of useful information on all things food business related, and Small Business Marketing Motivation, which is a place to learn and share experiences on social media and marketing for the small business owner. I'm also a member of a number of local networks and notice boards which give me a heads-up on local events and issues.

Twitter is a fast-paced, concise platform. It's an easy way to connect with your audience, allowing you to share quick pieces of information and photos in an effort to drive people back to your website. You only get 280 characters, so make them count.

If you're marketing on Twitter you need to have content that is enticing and eye-catching enough for people to stop and click through. People are normally scrolling quickly, so it needs to be something that will stop them in their tracks. Quotes, statistics or questions related to a link can work well. Photos, polls, gifs and short videos can help grab people's attention. Don't forget, though, that you're trying to build relationships with your followers. People will follow you because they like what you have to say, but they also want to engage in conversation.

Personally, I only use Twitter occasionally. I find that it can be quite a toxic platform at times so I'm quite cautious with the content I post. It's great for a bit of chit-chat during programmes like Bake Off, but in the main, it's a copy of what I've posted on Instagram. There are, however, 'hours' you can latch onto such as #WeddingHour for everything wedding related, #EssexHour for Essex-based businesses and so-on. The community side can be hugely important. Find those that are relevant to you and your brand and join the conversation. I've picked up a lot of business this way.

People searching for specific information will often check hashtags. Make some time to look at top stories and find out what's trending, and if it's relevant to your target audience, make sure you're tapping into it as well.

LinkedIn is specifically designed for business and professionals. It's mainly used to showcase work experience and professional thoughts. It's a good platform to use if you want to be recognised as an expert in your field.

YouTube is a great platform to use if you're doing something visually creative. Whilst you don't want to give away all your secrets you can share basic techniques and it's a great way to get your face known.

If you're creating YouTube videos, make sure there's purpose and value in your content and pay attention to the quality of the video you're sharing. It's a good way to launch yourself as an educator about your industry, but make sure your videos are of a decent quality.

Pinterest is very popular for brands with a tangible product such as clothing and food. It's a superficial platform, so every image needs to be high-quality and striking to make sure it stands out. Make sure your images click through to something that's relevant to the image you've posted.

Instagram is all about how visual your product is. Whilst I don't go crazy and photograph every moment of the working day, I will capture pictures and video of chocolate being tempered, and arrays of trays waiting to be capped off, or a tray of shiny truffles that I've just demoulded. I'll also keep an eye on what's trending and see if I can latch on to that. If there's a national day dedicated to a cocktail, or chocolate, then I'm all over it.

Hashtags are much more important on Instagram and will help you to be seen by more people. Don't just make something up and hope for the best. It needs to be pertinent. People do search for hashtags such as #FridayFeeling #ChocolateWeek and event-specific tags such as #BBCGoodFood.

One piece of advice I was given with hashtags is to capitalise each word. For the visually impaired this is vital when having things read out to them by a computer and for the general public it's easier to make sense of a hashtag composed of several words. For example #weareracing may make sense as you write it, but to someone who isn't clued up and wondering just what they're supposed to be wearing, #WeAreRacing makes a lot more sense. Susan Boyle's epic tweet would never have caused so much mirth if she'd capitalised each word.

I've never seen the benefit of using Snapchat myself, although I've seen it used very creatively by some businesses. A drinks manufacturer created a Halloween treasure hunt using geo-filters for people to discover creative cocktails using their products in various bars around London, for example.

Essentially, is your target audience using a particular social media platform? If so, you should be too. And once your business is on social media, then make sure you post regularly. It's an easy thing to forget when you're busy putting together a big order, but that means people will be forgetting who you are. Keep yourself front-of-mind with your followers. Have a plan, and plan your content. Don't just shove something out because you haven't posted in a while. Scheduling posts can be a useful way to make sure your posts are going out when your target market is online, but can also have its problems. If you've scheduled something light-hearted and a major disaster occurs, your post might be seen as insensitive or even insulting by the time it goes out.

Apps such as IFTTT (If This Then That) are great for helping manage social media. Although you can automatically post from one platform to another, what looks great on Facebook doesn't always translate to Instagram or Twitter. If you automatically post something on Instagram and then share it on Twitter, any images will show as a hyperlink. IFTTT has an option to post your Instagram photos as native pictures on Twitter, which is much more visually appealing to someone scrolling.

Advertising can work well if you have a call to action, but I've found that print media has become less and less important since I started the business. Having an ad in a local publication can be useful to remind people about your products, but be wary about advertising in glossy publications and national press. It's hugely expensive, so unless you think you'll get the return on your investment, then steer clear.

Advertising on social media can work, but people are becoming desensitised to all the 'noise' hidden amongst their Instagram stories and on their Facebook timeline, so make sure you do some research before parting with cash. Banner ads on websites run into the thousands of pounds, so much as it's tempting to have an ad running on a prestigious website, you'll need deep pockets.

Editorials make great PR. Try and develop a rapport with some local reporters and send them a press release whenever you've got something to shout about. If you've already written their copy for them, even better.

Similarly, link in to food journalists on Twitter and Instagram and try to tap into whatever they're posting about.

Don't be afraid to show off and be open about what you do. The best protection for your brand is being the first and being the best, so make sure that everyone knows it!

Kir Royale

The Kir Royale is a French cocktail, a variation on Kir. It consists of Crème de Cassis topped with champagne rather than the white wine used in traditional Kir. This aperitif is typically served in a flute glass.

Ingredients	o 9cl (3 oz) Champagne o 1cl (1/3 oz) Crème de Cassis
Preparation	Add the Crème de Cassis to the bottom of the glass then top up with Champagne.

CHAPTER SIXTEEN

Is the customer always right?

It goes without saying that at Choctails we strive for customer excellence. I know that we've got a great product, but I want to make the whole customer experience as great as possible so that people will want to continue to shop with us. Customer complaints are a way of life (albeit not a frequent one), but living by the expectation that "the customer is always right" is unrealistic.

We all make mistakes. I've received an order for two identical items and only shipped one. That kind of thing is easily dealt with and can be mitigated with closer attention to detail and better checks prior to shipping. Usually an apology and putting the situation right will suffice in such circumstances.

At Choctails we've had occasional instances (two) where the customer complains their chocolates don't taste of anything. This one is just a case of your word against theirs. We keep control batches for comparison, but a challenge to their palate would just result in confrontation and arguments. This is an example where you have to swallow your pride and either refund or replace. In both instances we've replaced with chocolates from the same batch and been told how much better the second box tasted.

I received a phone call during my early months telling me that the chocolates they'd purchased at the BBC Good Food show from us had bloomed. When I explained we only exhibited at local farmer's markets they hung up.

We've had an instance where someone complained that the chocolates in the Full Monty were smaller than those in the Classic Collection they'd purchased in the past. Given that they're exactly the same chocolates, made using exactly the same moulds, I wasn't sure how that could have happened.

There are many instances where I know people are trying it on in order to get a freebie. In a lot of cases I calmly explain why that can't possibly be the case, but what happens when you're not sure if the complaint is genuine or not? 'The order didn't arrive' is a prime example of this. It's a rare occurrence and although we now track all our shipments, if that proves inconclusive we generally give them the benefit of the doubt, but here's a scenario we came across:

A customer orders a box of chocolates. The billing and the shipping information is identical. The purchaser and the recipient are identical. The chocolates are dispatched via Royal Mail and the confirmation email is sent to the customer. A week later the customer contacts me to tell me that the chocolates have not arrived. An investigation reveals nothing concrete, so we conclude that the chocolates have been lost in the post and therefore offer to send a replacement box.

The customer responds:

> "Thank you Hilary, my parents are very elderly and I wanted them to have a nice surprise. I am overseas, an aid worker, and life is tough.

Please can you keep me in the loop as to when the choices [*I assume this is an auto-correct of choccies*] go out and when they may receive them?

I have been waiting patiently for their hearts to be uplifted. They are amazing parents who will love this surprise of nice chocolates....

Thank you."

Something didn't quite ring true when I read this. If the chocolates were meant as a gift, why was the billing and shipping information identical, and why were they addressed to the person who placed the order? Would my parents open a package addressed to me if I was away? Absolutely not! If I'd given them permission to open my mail, then they would have done so, but with no gift message in the box they would have no idea it was for them.

Against my better judgement I sent a replacement box, this time using Royal Mail Tracked, which tracks the delivery progress but doesn't require a signature.

A week later, I received the following email:

> "Hi Hilary, the chocolates have still not arrived
> at my parents house in Marshfield. Maybe I
> should have a refund? Very disappointed."

My first instincts were right. I sent back a screen shot of proof of delivery and explained that I was unable to refund the cost as it clearly showed the chocolates had been delivered.

It's often useful to talk to other people when you receive a customer complaint. There are Facebook communities where you can connect with other people in your industry to share advice and feedback. I'm a member of The Food Hub on Facebook, which is a mine of information for food entrepreneurs and there's usually someone who has come across a similar scenario if you're unsure about how to handle a specific complaint.

There are some complaints which give you a cold shiver when you receive them, such as this one:

> "A friend bought your chocolate as a gift for my birthday but I was disappointed to find a hair in it. Not what I was expecting."

As a food producer, this gives you that kicked-in-the-stomach feeling. How can such a thing happen when we're so careful to keep hair tied back at all times and use hairnets whenever we're in production? I decided to investigate further:

> "Thank you for bringing this to our attention. We obviously need to look into how this has happened. Would you be able to tell me whether it was a production or packing error, and who purchased the chocolates so that we can trace it back to when the chocolates were made and packaged?"

I received no further contact from the customer, which I thought was odd, but then a few weeks later I bumped into some fellow chocolatiers who asked if I'd received an email complaining about a hair in my chocolate. It turned out I wasn't the only one. In fact there were at least four other chocolatiers who had received the same email. What alerted one company to the fraud was the fact that the chocolatier is bald …..

As soon as our products were launched in John Lewis, the number of complaints increased and it was blatantly obvious they had just seen our chocolates on the shelves and were trying to get a freebie out of us. One example was that someone claimed to have purchased a box in June but only just opened them. We didn't even start production for JLR until July.

But let me ask you, if you purchased an item from a store and found it was faulty, who would you complain to? Personally, I'd go back to the store and not direct to the supplier. It is altogether possible that some would come direct to us with a complaint, however. Here are two variations on the same theme:

"good morning

i purchased a box of your cocktail truffles 246g from john lewis and the box was missing 4 of the truffles

179

> i appreciate this fed back as i am a loyal
> customer of yours"

This was received about a week after our products were launched into John Lewis, and the email was from someone who's name didn't appear on any of our purchase order records. So I was confused as to how they were a loyal customer.

In addition, none of our boxes weigh 246g, and why identify it by weight and not by the name of the collection? The closest was our After Dinner Collection and with twelve spaces in the box we would have noticed four missing. In fact we notice if there's even one missing.

The second one was a little more believable:

> "To Whom This May Concern,
>
> I would like to draw your attention to a slightly embarrassing situation that happened to my wife.
>
> Towards the back end of November she bought one of your Full Monty Boxes from John Lewis to find missing chocolates. I am

unsure whether this is the responsibility of yourself of John Lewis but she informs me the purchase wasn't made under any sort of discount and the packaging was immaculate and sealed and she is one of those sticklers for boxes / perfection.

The embarrassing part was when my difficult mother made a recent comment about us being hungry before we delivered her gifts to her and informed us of the half empty box of chocolates.

Unfortunately because of the nature of the product and the fact it was a gift she didn't keep the receipt so I can't add any more detail to this. I thought I would make you aware of this because we have bought this particular box of chocolates before for ourselves and two other people as gifts and we have been very happy and usually are endorsers of your product as would be foodies."

Here's the thing. Our boxes are packed by hand and go through a number of checks during the packing process.

All our different varieties are boxed up in trays of forty two – not because it's the answer to life, the universe and everything, but because the storage trays hold six rows of seven chocolates. The packing table holds seven rows of six vac-formed trays. For this reason, when batch packing, we always pack forty two of a collection at a time. If there's any discrepancy between the production team (me) and the packing team (me or Simon), it's picked up immediately.

Once the forty two collections have been picked, we then do a visual check – any gaps are immediately obvious – before closing and sealing the interior packing.

At this point we weigh every box before it's film wrapped. At 10g a chocolate, any short-filled boxes would stand out.

Of course, not all customer complainants are happy to leave it alone. Even having put a situation right, there's nothing to stop a customer writing a bad review on various online platforms. It's much easier for someone to post up a bad review than it is for you to have it taken down, even if the customer hasn't purchased via that particular marketplace. If it's one bad review amidst a raft of good ones, the chances are that no one will notice, or dismiss it altogether. If you have the option to write a public reply, then do so, but be polite and stick to the facts.

Never, ever, get into a public slanging match. If someone's intent on trolling you, then report them, block them and move on. I know how difficult it is to ignore and not to take it personally, but it's the best way forward.

Don't rush to refund or replace as soon as you receive a complaint. Investigate it thoroughly first and be absolutely sure it's genuine. If you're not sure, but want to make a gesture of goodwill then money-off vouchers are a good solution. It means they need to purchase from you again to realise the benefit.

Essentially, these people don't want to purchase your product at the price you're selling it for. They want you to sell your product to them at a lower rate, which means they want you to work for less money.

There are genuine complaints and feedback which do need to be investigated, however. The hair in the chocolate email, even though it turned out not to be genuine, had me stopping production to assess my production and packing methods.

A complaint about our Mocktails collection, even though the product was consumed a month after the best before date, led us to withdraw the entire collection from sale for six months whilst we investigated the issue.

What I would say, is keep fastidious production records, particularly if you're stocked in a big name retailer. Yes, it takes time, but it covers your back in the case of any complaints and allows you to check back to see if they might have a genuine reason to complain, or if they're just after a freebie.

All the ingredients we use are logged into the Raw Ingredients folder. We note the name of the product and who supplied it, where it was purchased from, the date the product was received or purchased and the best before date indicated on the packet. When the product is opened we make a note of the date to allow full traceability in the event of any issues. We also make a note of the date the ingredient was used by once the packet is empty.

We keep daily production records, noting down what was made on each date, as well as the air temperature and humidity in the kitchen, and whether we used the air-conditioning or not. We record details such as the weight of the mould throughout the process, re-weighing as the chocolate is added, the filling added, and then once it's capped off. If the weights are too far off from the master list, for example if the first chocolate layer is too thick, then the batch doesn't make it to the sales floor.

As each Choctail is boxed up after production, we note down the name of the chocolate, the batch number and the production date. As each collection is boxed up, we note down the date it was ordered and the order number along with the quantity of boxes being made up. Each collection is given its own batch number. The best before date is assigned as six months after the production date of the product with the shortest shelf life.

This amount of detail may seem excessive, but in the case of a complaint it makes the investigation process so much easier.

Sea Breeze

A Sea Breeze is a vodka-based cocktail usually consumed during the summer months. The drink may be shaken in order to create a foamy surface. It follows the classic cocktail principle of balancing strong with weak and sweet with sour.

Ingredients	○ 4cl Vodka ○ 12cl Cranberry Juice ○ 3cl Grapefruit Juice
Preparation	Build all the ingredients in a highball glass filled with ice. Garnish with a lime wedge.

CHAPTER SEVENTEEN

Retailing

We'd had a couple of forays into retailing with our old branding. Our first encounter was with Williams & Griffin, a local department store, who told us we needed to sort out our packaging before they would consider stocking us on their shelves. We suggested some alternative solutions and each time we were met with a different excuse. The first year it was 'We've already placed our Christmas orders. Call again next year.' I clarified when Christmas ordering was usually done and diarised to call in April the following year, only to be told they wouldn't be taking on any new suppliers until the imminent store refurbishments were completed.

Our second retail encounter was a local garden centre who have a big Christmas section every year featuring local producers. That was a much more favourable experience. I had a chat, let them sample some chocolates and walked away with a £750 order. At the time I thought I was going to expire with the volume of chocolate I was going to have to make!

As we have a few local stores with a chocolate pick-and-mix counter I offer all my chocolates for sale by the kilo, and so I also had stockists in Ipswich and Harwich. With this option people have no idea who has supplied the chocolates to the store and even though it can be a profitable partnership, it does little to promote your own brand. That's the kind of thing you need to vocalise on social media.

Our new branding was turning a few heads and getting more interest from our local retailers, but then something happened that I really wasn't expecting. I received an email from the confectionery buyer at Harvey Nichols who was interested in us as a potential supplier. I must admit, I initially thought it was a scam or someone playing an elaborate joke on me, but after half an hour of research I discovered it was the genuine article and we really had received a direct approach from Harvey Nichols.

The negotiations with Harvey Nichols took several months. The biggest issue with buyers in a store like this is that they're very busy, and whilst they're a big priority for you and at the top of your list, the converse isn't true. With a hundred different current and potential suppliers trying to get in touch with them on a daily basis, you have to be patient and a little tenacious. Don't bombard them, but make sure you keep on their radar. Avoid trying to contact them on a Monday as that's the day they're generally going through weekly sales figures and busy with meetings. Avoid Friday afternoons as they're often gathering information and figures in preparation for Monday's meetings.

Other than having to wait a few months before things progressed, Harvey Nichols had to be the easiest negotiation I've experienced to date. They accepted our wholesale prices and minimum order quantities without question, and we were in store by October.

That same year we were also stocked in Selfridges. This had been via a completely different route in that we had been approached by a distribution company and not the end retailer. With distributors there are the good guys and there are the bad guys. Trebuchet turned out to be the latter. We spent several weeks going backwards and forwards on price. They asked us to quote on bigger and bigger volumes to try and get us to reduce our costs. The promise of the eye-watering volumes never materialised. Our contract said we would be paid 50% on receipt of order and the remainder when we delivered our first shipment and although we eventually got paid it was in increasingly smaller chunks and several months removed from the terms were expecting.

Going through a distributor can have its advantages. They know all the pitfalls of dealing with their clients and can guide you through how to package and label your shipment. From the client's point of view they are dealing with one distributor in place of a hundred producers. However, the distributor also needs to make money, and so will add their percentage to your price, meaning you will need to reduce your own price point even further to maintain a reasonable wholesale price to the end client.

Economies of scale can play a factor, particularly with packaging volumes. However, if you're an artisan producer making every chocolate by hand, the per-chocolate cost of making 1,000 chocolates isn't going to be much different to the per-chocolate cost of making 100 chocolates. And if you need to enlist help in delivering the volumes, that impacts your bottom line.

Although our promise of eye-watering volumes for Selfridges didn't materialise, the result was that we were stocked in all the Selfridges UK stores. Our first payment was six months overdue, and the balance came through in a series of small instalments but we did eventually get paid in full.

That wasn't the biggest scam I dealt with that year, though. I was approached by a wholesale company based in Scotland asking for price lists and trade application forms. They placed an order for 350 boxes on 30 day terms and when those arrived their customers were so impressed that they ordered a further 300 boxes. That was the last I heard from them. It turned out the trader ran up £250,000 of unpaid debt in six months. According to an article published in the Daily Record on 17 February 2015, six companies raised actions against Richard Faith and his business for more than £50,000. He had ordered a wide range of goods from firms across the UK including kitchen units, washing machines, vacuum cleaners and food products. Companies such as Brake Brothers, HillHouse Quarry Group and Rexel were defrauded.

With hindsight, I should not have shipped the second order until the first had been paid. With even more hindsight, I should not have shipped anything without being paid. I had no idea who this company was, after all. The fact that they were so evasive as to who their end client was should have rung alarm bells. The fact that the manager signed herself 'Liz Brown' in the initial email and 'Liz Smith' thereafter should have stood out like a glaringly sore thumb. Yes, I was incredibly stupid. Yes, I was incredibly naive. I let the excitement of another high volume order cloud my judgement. It's too easy to get carried away because you think you're about to hit the big time.

That was the last time I offered 30 day terms to anyone other than our established clients. Our terms and conditions were tightened up by a lawyer and we insist on a proforma invoice with all new clients. If they're genuine, they won't have a problem with paying up front.

The Faith in the Future incident had taken some of the shine off the glittering prize that was being stocked in every Selfridges and Harvey Nichols store in the UK, but once we visited a few stores and saw ourselves on the shelves, the excitement returned. Friends began tweeting photos of our boxes wherever they saw them. It's such a proud moment to see your own handiwork on the shelves of such prestigious retailers.

The following March I met the buyer for Harvey Nichols again, with a view to us being restocked the following Christmas. Sales had been good throughout the festive period, and instore tasting events had proved worthwhile. The main problem, however, had been their lack of exclusivity.

The exclusivity factor can be a good bargaining chip with a big name retailer. When Harvey Nichols held their 2014

Christmas launch event to introduce their new brands, most of the press had already seen our products the week before at the Selfridges launch and thus the impact was diminished.

Consequently, I was asked to produce a Christmas Collection that Harvey Nichols would have exclusivity on. I already had four seasonal flavours that I'd been working on over the last couple of years; Sloe Gin, Christmas Pudding; Mulled Wine, and a Port and Stilton. The last one sounds crazy, but it was inspired by a dessert I was given when having dinner with some friends. We were given a chocolate tart with a thin layer of Stilton cheese on top, served with a glass of Port. The flavours worked so well together, that I just had to put it into a truffle.

Whilst everyone was enjoying Easter Eggs, I was busy developing Christmas chocolates. It's not easy to source Winter Pimm's in April, or to put yourself in mind of winter drinks and desserts when the evenings are getting lighter, but you'd be amazed just how far ahead a chocolatier will be working. With flavour development and pitching to retailers, it often feels as if we're focussed on Christmas for most of the year.

By May, we had twelve chocolates we were happy with. Coker Brand Design suggested we call it a Festive Collection instead of just limiting it to a Christmas Collection. Harvey Nichols were happy, and we were back on their shelves the following October.

Being stocked by a major retailer one year doesn't guarantee you will be again. They like to rotate who they're stocking and a lot of that will depend on who's hot right now, and what's on trend.

I've also found that I constantly need to be on the look-out for potential new retailers. My stockist in Harwich had to close her deli suddenly due to personal reasons. My stockist in Ipswich could no longer afford the business rates and disappeared almost overnight. Other stockists wanted to ring the changes after a while and rested us for a year.

I tried to think laterally as well when looking for places to retail my chocolates. Flowers and chocolates. Wine and chocolates. Cocktail bars. Hotels.

It was our local boutique hotel who inspired me to create a Mocktails Collection. They'd specifically asked for non-alcoholic chocolates to offer as an in-room package. I began with a simple range which included things like an orange truffle, a mint truffle, salted caramel, but somehow it didn't feel like it fitted in with our core brand. Eventually I developed the Mocktails range so that we had a completely alcohol-free collection for those who can't or don't want to have alcohol in their chocolate.

Trade shows can be a good way to initiate conversations with retailers, but I've also picked up business from a number of consumer shows. In the main these will be independent regional stores, but a show such as the BBC Good Food Show will usually have its share of buyers wandering around.

It was at a local food festival that I finally got my opportunity to pitch for Williams & Griffin. The store had finally been refurbished and rebranded as Fenwick

Colchester instead of a regional brand. The Assistant Food Buyer introduced herself to me. She was on a fact-finding trip and even though I was streaming with cold and not feeling particularly enthusiastic, I managed to pull myself together for a productive chat. We were in store two months later.

I've exhibited at a few trade shows over the years and done reasonably well out of them, but there are a few things to keep in mind when choosing your trade show. I exhibited at a Local Flavours event in Norfolk where the majority of buyers were looking to buy local, and unfortunately Essex wasn't local enough for most of them.

The Speciality and Fine Food Fair at Olympia is one of the biggest trade shows in the UK but with that comes a large stand fee and sample budget. I'd exhibited three years in a row and decided that I needed a year away from the chaos. It's three long, foot-sore days. Unlike a consumer show, you have no immediate sales to show for your efforts. Once the show is over you then have the logistical nightmare that is stand break down at 5pm on a Tuesday afternoon when thousands of exhibitors are trying to do the same thing. Having taken a year away from the show, I almost didn't rebook for 2017 but eventually thought I would give it one more go.

This time I was a bit more savvy with potential buyers. I had goody bags but made sure they were only for those who seemed genuinely interested. By now I had developed a better instinct as to who was genuine and not just after a goody bag. There were plenty of samples on the stand for everyone else. As always I made sure to make notes and exchange business cards ready to follow up as soon as I got back.

The dynamic of the show changes over the three days. Sunday is mostly independent retailers who are often visiting with their family, so there will be a lot of children around. Monday is for the larger retailers who can afford to send their buyers to the show for the day as part of their working week. Tuesday is when the big guns are out.

I was hugely excited by the conversation I had with John Lewis and they were one of the first to come back to me when I sent out my 'lovely to meet you at the show' email. I sent a sample set and then a follow-up email a couple of weeks later to be told they hadn't had an opportunity to review our product but would in due course.

Christmas came and went and still we heard nothing, until April 2018 when the buyer contacted me to progress the conversation. This was a very different conversation to my previous retail negotiations. Big retailers are all about profit and that means that you need to cut your margins in order to meet their costs. And when I say cut your margins, I mean slash them.

Having negotiated to a point where the end client was happy and we were relatively okay with our final price point, we were asked to go via a distributor. Yes, it was going to make our logistics a lot easier, but it also meant a further cut to our profit margins.

For the last few years we'd been happy supplying local independent shops, with an idea to supplying bigger stores in the future. We'd been following a classic low-volume-high-margin approach which was making us a reasonable profit. However, we always had a dream to make it big, and so when John Lewis came calling, we were all ears. We were going to be in John Lewis! This was going to be the deal which made us a household name and meant that Simon could give up the IT work and come and work with me full time.

Long Island Iced Tea

Robert "Rosebut" Butt claims to have invented the Long Island Iced Tea as an entry in a contest to create a new mixed drink with Triple Sec in 1972 while he worked at the Oak Beach Inn on Long Island, New York.

A slightly different drink is claimed to have been invented in the 1920s during prohibition by an "Old Man Bishop" and perfected by his son. The drink included whiskey and maple syrup and varied quantities of the five liquors rather than the modern one with cola and five equal portions of the five liquors.

Ingredients	
	o 1.5cl Tequila
	o 1.5cl Vodka
	o 1.5cl White Rum
	o 1.5cl Triple Sec
	o 1.5cl Gin
	o 2.5cl Lemon Juice
	o 3.0cl Gomme Syrup
	o 1 dash of Cola

Preparation	Add all the ingredients to a highball glass filled with ice. Stir gently. Garnish with a lemon spiral and serve with a straw.

CHAPTER EIGHTEEN

Playing With The Big Boys

The initial enquiry we based our pricing on for John Lewis Retail (JLR) was for 7,170 boxes (101,420 individual truffles) and 8,890 chocolate bars. Over the years, I'd discovered that a comfortable production volume for me was 500-600 truffles in a day. I knew I could double that volume but it left me with time for little else during the day.

Once we'd got the sign off, the forecast volumes we received were for 7,800 boxes (110,800 individual truffles) and 9,540 bars in five drops, one each month from August through to December. We were also told we would be in all fifty stores and online, which was rare for a new supplier.

Sign-off wasn't received until June and I wasn't going to start production until we'd got everything in writing. We were going to need to produce and pack around 6,000 truffles and 400 chocolate bars each week from the beginning of July through to the end of November.

We thought about taking on an extra pair of hands, but that would have cut our profit margins dramatically. Also, we couldn't employ someone until we'd received the purchase order and knew for definite that we'd have need of the extra person. The paperwork didn't materialise until the beginning of June, meaning I now didn't have time to train someone up. Automation was out of the question. It was a huge cost and we didn't have the space for the machinery.

The only thing for it was that we were going to have to work ridiculously hard. Simon told me all I had to do was focus on making chocolate and he would take care of everything else – meals, housework, laundry, and packing the chocolates into boxes. We knew it was going to be hard work and we knew it was going to take its toll on us physically, mentally and emotionally.

My initial plan was to spend a week making white chocolate, a week on milk chocolate and a week on dark chocolate, so that I only had one type of chocolate to temper each week, and could reuse the moulds as soon as I demoulded a batch of truffles. That worked really well for me; however, when it came to packing the boxes, it meant Simon had to wait almost three weeks before he could pack anything other than chocolate bars. As a consequence we had to put out a desperate plea to four loyal friends to help with packing and wrapping boxes in the final week so that we could deliver drop one on time.

I subsequently changed my work pattern so that I would spend two days on white chocolate, truffles one day and bars the next, followed by two days on milk and two days on dark, meaning that Simon could keep on top of the packing. Of course, it's not quite as simple as two days on each type of chocolate, as the truffle filling needs to set overnight before it's capped off, so it would mean an early start to cap off the white chocolate bars on a Wednesday morning before starting on the milk chocolate, and a similar routine on a Friday to cap off the milk chocolate bars before starting on the dark chocolate. Sunday was spent capping off the dark chocolate bars, finishing any decoration (such as the milk chocolate drizzle on the ginger truffles), and then washing moulds (all 295 of them).

My four-times-a-week morning runs were cut to three and I reduced the distance so that I was only out for forty minutes at a time instead of an hour. I gave up alcohol completely as I had to be up and firing on all cylinders every day. I couldn't even stop for PopMaster.

We were up at six every morning, seven days a week, unless we could afford a cheeky lie-in until seven on a Sunday. Most days we would manage to get to bed before eleven, but there were several occasions when we were still up at midnight.

I'm not entirely sure how I kept myself motivated for those months. I just had to keep the production levels up, no question. There were days when I hadn't tempered the chocolate properly because I was rushing, and only half the batch came out of the moulds. There were days when I piped the ganache filling in before it was cool enough and ended up with air holes in the top of a couple of trays worth of chocolates. There were many days when a proportion of the chocolate bars had cooled too slowly resulting in an unattractive bloom.

The long hot summer of 2018 did nothing to help our cause. We have a portable air conditioning unit which has been more than adequate in keeping the kitchen cool for the last few years, but suddenly the temperatures soared and the dining room was now getting dangerously warm. We dug our old fan out of the loft and had it sitting on ice packs to keep our storage space cool.

Keylink phoned to say they wouldn't be shipping chocolate during the very hot weather in case it harmed the chocolate, so my order was going to be late. I begged them to send it anyway as I couldn't afford to wait. Luckily my DPD driver knew me well enough to know what was in the boxes, and made sure my deliveries were as early as possible so they weren't sitting in the van all day.

And then the aircon unit failed. It was a Wednesday morning and it gave out a suspicious clunk. Simon tried to get it working again but had to give up. I began to worry.

Simon immediately went online and sourced an industrial-sized unit which was going to keep the entire downstairs area cold and was on a next day delivery. When the unit hadn't turned up by Thursday afternoon I started to panic. After a phone call Simon told me it wasn't actually going to arrive until Monday. That was the point at which I completely lost it and had a full-on melt-down.

Once I'd vented my spleen and then collapsed into a sobbing heap I had no option but to pick myself up and soldier on. I had to keep making the chocolate and hope everything would turn out okay. There was no way I could lose four production days just because I hadn't got air conditioning.

With volume production, don't be surprised if your costs exceed your initial forecast. I found I needed additional storage space for my moulds. That meant a second racking trolley which I hadn't budgeted for. The company I buy my cardboard packing boxes from found they were out of stock of my usual size of box, but had an alternative that was slightly bigger and therefore a little more expensive.

I'd budgeted for couriering our deliveries, but the volumes were so large that we needed to palletise everything. We couldn't just forage for an available pallet or two as they had to be food-grade pallets. There was no way we could palletise the drop ourselves as we would never have got it out of the front door, and leaving the chocolates outside wasn't an option, so that also meant we had the additional costs of getting the courier to palletise it for us.

The list went on ….

Drop one was delivered on time thanks to our team of helpers and a few very late nights, and then we were straight in to drop two, based on the forecast we'd been given. We were now into a daily routine which worked well for both of us.

I would be in the kitchen by 7:15 if I was running, and 6:30 if I wasn't, and have the chocolate ready tempered before breakfast. I would then be fully focussed on coating chocolate trays until I was called for lunch. After lunch I would finish coating the remaining trays and then prepare and pipe the truffle fillings until dinner. Meal times would move to accommodate how much I had left to do, but if I wasn't going to be finished by a sensible dinner time I would continue piping the fillings afterwards, before washing up and cleaning down.

After a quick al fresco breakfast, Simon would pack a batch of one of our 12-chocolate collections (a batch being forty two boxes for the reasons I mentioned earlier). He would then move on to his day job (fortunately working from home and on reduced hours) from 10am until 5pm. After that he would pack a second batch of collections before he made dinner. Once we'd eaten I would clean down whilst Simon film-wrapped all the boxes and then we would have an hour or so wrapping chocolate bars together before collapsing into bed. Weekends were Simon's days for packing and wrapping the Full Monty boxes.

The distribution company then contacted me with a change to the forecast. JLR wanted to put us at the till points, which was fantastic. It would mean two drops instead of four with an increase in volumes, which wasn't so fantastic. I was already having doubts that I would be able to achieve the December forecast. Simon and I had a heated discussion over what we could achieve.

We initially thought the volumes they were proposing were on top of the forecast volumes we'd already been given and Simon knew that would be impossible for me to achieve. After we went back to the distribution company for clarification we found out this would be replacing the original forecast. Even so, it was a big ask. It was something I really wanted to achieve but Simon was, as ever, my voice of reason. He could see how hard I was pushing myself already and knew the extra work would take its toll on my health and wellbeing.

Eventually I pushed back. The numbers JLR had proposed for the next drop were achievable in the timescales I had been given, but the volumes for the final drop weren't, so I went back with what I could achieve and by when. JLR agreed to our numbers.

Don't ever be scared to negotiate over production volumes. If you're up front and tell your retailer what you can achieve in the timescales, they'll be a lot happier than if you say yes and then fail to deliver. I do occasionally revisit the numbers in my head and wonder if I could have achieved the final numbers (the answer's always no, by the way), but I'd be beating myself up even more if I'd straight out said no to being at the till points, or yes to their forecast and then fallen short.

During this time the price of chocolate went up. By the time we made our final drop we were making a loss on our chocolate bars. On top of all that, we were on sixty day terms – no negotiation. By the way, that's sixty days from the date they accept the order into the JLR warehouse and not sixty days from the date it leaves us to be palletised and then shipped to the distributor.

The one big lesson I've learned from all of this is that if you go from supplying the independents with a high quality product you're probably going to be unhappy with your volume product. My quality checks weren't quite as vigorous. I was allowing more than the occasional chocolate through that had air bubbles in it because I didn't want to have to make another tray, when previously it would have gone into the spoiled chocolate pot. You may need to use lower quality ingredients, or make other compromises you might not be comfortable with in order to see a profit. If you then go back to the independents your regular consumers might not be happy with a lower quality product.

If you're going to make compromises on costs, then where do you compromise? It's tempting to look at cheaper distribution, for example, but that's one area where you absolutely shouldn't compromise. I've witnessed a MyHermes driver throwing boxes into his van after picking them up from a local collection point. That's not how I want my business to be treated, so I'm happy to pay more for a company with a good reputation and a guarantee that everything's going to arrive on time and intact.

For me, I wasn't going to compromise on the quality of my ingredients, so I had to rely on volume discounts. I regularly had two hundred kilos of chocolate piled up in my hallway looking for a storage space.

I'd made some savings on bulk buying my boxes. I was getting small but significant volume discounts on my ingredients. I found some cushion pads that were two pence cheaper than our regular supplier, but they were half a centimetre too big for the box and needed to be trimmed down. We'd saved some money there, but not time.

Finally, on 14 November 2018, we could breathe. Our final drop had been collected by the courier. My house could go back to being a home again, instead of a warehouse, and I could slow down a little. Over the previous five months we'd had two days off (not consecutively) and a further two nights out.

I couldn't slow down too much, though. I had the BBC Good Food Show in less than a fortnight and some local Christmas shows to prepare for. I hadn't even started making Festive Collections, which we usually have ready online by October.

We tried to renegotiate with JLR to continue to be stocked for the Spring and Summer in 2019. However, they wanted similar volumes to Autumn-Winter, which wasn't sustainable for us, and they wouldn't agree a twelve pence price increase on the chocolate bars to allow us to at least break even on our costs.

Sales figures hadn't been forthcoming, so we weren't sure if the projected volumes were going to be realistic in terms of sales. We knew for a fact that chocolate sales drop off dramatically in January with an uplift around Valentine's Day, Mothers' Day and Easter, but volumes are nothing close those we achieve during the run up to Christmas. We know that the Mocktails Collection sales are a lot lower than those of our alcoholic ranges. We know for a fact that the Gin chocolate bar sells twice as fast as the Irish Cream both online and at a show, but without their sales figures to corroborate, we were unable to propose an alternate forecast.

At this point we concluded that this wasn't where we wanted the business to be. Within days of the final drop both Simon and I came down with heavy colds which lasted us until Christmas and then flared up again in February. I'd missed out on a number of favourite local Christmas shows and events because I had neither the energy or the stock available. We'd both missed out on a lot of social events and weekends away because we were just too busy. It was time to get the work-life balance a little more level.

As I mentioned earlier, if you have any inkling of supplying big volume you should look at all the numbers and costs, then set things up so these are already factored in. How you set your company up pre-launch has a huge effect on your options down the road. There are some brands that have managed to make the switch but most find it very hard or not viable.

Moving to high volume is less about the quality of the product. Provenance isn't necessarily important when doing the weekly shop. This is the point where you need to look beyond the product you make and focus on margin and profit. It's not easy to go from making amazing food at home to being in 1500 or even 50 stores nationally. If you want big sales you need deep pockets. Crowd funding is an option, but that seems to have lost its momentum over the last few years, with a number of companies failing to make their crowdfunding targets. Many artisan food companies are doing very well but think the grass is greener on the other side, as we did. In many instances it's not the case.

Dual branding is another option. We often toyed with the idea of bringing in automation so that we could mass-produce Choctails for the high volume retailers, but to run that alongside a 'Handmade by Hilary Delamare' line aimed at the independents.

There are other routes to funding volume distribution, of course. At one event in 2013 I took a shared corner pitch with a young girl who made fabulous cakes. Her name was Alana Spencer, the winner of The Apprentice in 2016. Being Lord Sugar's business partner has taken her business from the charming 'Narna's Cakes' to the hugely successful 'Ridiculously Rich by Alana'. The reality TV route is always an option if you want to take your business to the next level, and had I wished to carry on with the volume sales option you may well have found me appearing on Dragon's Den.

Brandy Alexander

Some say the Brandy Alexander was created at the time of the wedding of Princess Mary and Viscount Lascelles in 1922. Drama critic Alexander Woollcott claimed it was named after him. Other sources say it was named after Russian Tsar Alexander II. The drink was possibly named after Troy Alexander, a bartender at Rector's in New York. The cocktail is known to have been John Lennon's favourite drink. He was introduced to it by Harry Nilsson in the midst of Lennon's so-called "lost weekend".

Ingredients	o 3cl Cognac o 3cl Crème de Cacao o 3cl Fresh Cream
Preparation	Shake the ingredients together and strain into a chilled cocktail glass. Sprinkle with fresh ground nutmeg.

CHAPTER NINETEEN

What next?

Having decided that big retail wasn't where I wanted to be, the big question is where do I want to be? The whole landscape of food shows has changed in recent years, and the few shows I've exhibited at this year haven't been as profitable as they have been in the past. However, moving back towards regular shows and local, independent retailers is definitely appealing.

I recently had an approach from a major high street confectioner who wanted to put our chocolates into their packaging. It may not come to anything as I suspect volumes will be too high and margins will be too tight, but it's worth a conversation at least.

I've been enjoying doing some product development, learning some different techniques and some slightly different products – still on the same cocktail theme of course. The pimped up "Mars Bars" went down a treat, once I'd mastered nougat.

Chocolate demos are always entertaining for me to do, not least because you're in front of a live audience and nowhere to hide if anything goes wrong. It's not easy to bluff your way through a batch of burned caramel, although you can turn it into a troubleshooting exercise. It's a great way to engage with the public for an hour.

I've hosted a few chocolate workshops that have been so much fun for everyone involved. I would love to offer this as an option on our web site, but my home kitchen isn't really suitable for it, and I've not yet found a local venue I'm happy with.

Having done the rounds of the local WI groups, I discovered I love going out and talking about my journey. Evening talks weren't a viable option last year, but with a more relaxed workload, it means I can make myself available to doing more of this.

With a little more time on my hands I can finally look into getting my YouTube channel up and running with some 'how to' videos.

It could be that I follow in my mother's footsteps after all and go into teaching chocolate skills. Perhaps the careers officer had it right all along.

One thing is for certain, I'll continue to experiment, tinker and be creative.

So now tell me I'll never find a career which combines art and science.

Strawberry Daiquiri

Daiquiri is a family of cocktails whose main ingredients are rum, citrus and sugar or other sweetener.

Ingredients	o 4.5cl White Rum o 2.5cl Lime Juice o 4.5cl Strawberry Puree
Preparation	Shake all the ingredients over ice. Strain into a chilled cocktail glass.

ACKNOWLEDGEMENTS

Thank you to the following people, without whom none of this would even exist, let alone be possible:

To Simon for giving me the self-belief that I could take this journey, and for having the crazy idea in the first place.

To my stepson Charlie for wanting to show my chocolates off to his work experience colleagues.

To Beverley at the UK Chocolate Academy for teaching me so much more than I thought I'd ever know about chocolate.

To Coker Brand Design (Simon, Jenny and Rebecca) for the stunning visual identity and for taking us in a more focussed direction.

To Clive for all the legal advice.

To Di-onne, Miles, Trisha and Zoe for stepping in to help us pack our first John Lewis order.

To my brother Christopher for the help in editing this book.

To Matt for suggesting I write the thing in the first place.

To BBC Radio Two for providing me with some company and great music every day.

An enormous thank you to every single person who's ever bought Choctails at a market, show, direct from me, online, from a retailer, as a trade-off. Without you, absolutely none of this would have happened.

To everyone who's liked, shared or commented on any one of our social media posts.

To you, for buying and reading this book.

All cocktail recipes are courtesy of Difford's Guide and the International Bartender's Guide via Wikipedia.

The 'A brief history of chocolate' chapter was developed from content on History.com and Wikipedia.

The 'Modern chocolate production' chapter was developed from content on Confectionery News, Wikipedia and The World Atlas of Chocolate.

Printed in Great Britain
by Amazon